THE SWAN LAND AND CATTLE COMPANY, LTD.

THE SWAN LAND
AND CATTLE
COMPANY, LTD.

BY HARMON ROSS MOTHERSHEAD

University of Oklahoma Press
Norman

International Standard Book Number: 0–8061–0973–4
Library of Congress Catalog Card Number: 79–160501
Copyright 1971 by the University of Oklahoma Press, Publishing Division
of the University. Composed and printed at Norman, Oklahoma, U.S.A.,
by the University of Oklahoma Press.
First edition.

To Ellen

PREFACE

MANY MEN tried to exploit the grassland of the Great Plains once it had been wrested from the native occupants. The vastness of that virgin land demanded more than the efforts of one man; it demanded collective action. Some men chose a political structure, the stockmen's association; others chose an economic structure, the cattle company. This story is an example of the latter.

The period following the Civil War in the United States was one of rapid economic and industrial growth. Industrial expansion was dependent upon a seemingly unlimited supply of natural resources and sufficient capital to exploit them. Resources were readily available in America, but capital was not.

The 1880's were a period of virtually unrestrained private enterprise in America. Corporations, trusts, and other combinations of corporate enterprise, the typical economic organizations of the period for large-scale developments, appeared ideally suited to raising capital and organizing the industrial complex. Natural resources were at once the assets upon which organizations were built and the object of exploitation of the organizations. Capital thus created was multiplied by pyramiding companies to begin a remarkable economic expansion.

The uninhibiting atmosphere that prevailed throughout the 1870's and 1880's gave birth to a generation of ambitious self-made men—men who by hard work, foresight, shrewdness, boldness, personality, or a tinge of larceny, or by combinations of such qualities, rose from obscurity to positions of influence, power, and prominence, locally, nationally, and in some instances internationally.

Capital was applied to opportunity by some shrewd men who almost without exception seized upon the same tool: the joint-stock company. Empires, many of them only on paper, were built. Some prospered, some failed, but in all instances the movement was toward greater control, increased size, and monopolization. Beef, timber, steel, railroads, mining—nearly all activities associated with the West —were included. No door was closed to opportunity.

In terms of pure capital, the West itself provided a very real part of the economic growth—gold and silver, the most secure of all assets. In the decade after the Civil War the discovery of precious metals, the building of railroads, and the growth of industry wrought great changes in the financial world. By the 1880's the western range-cattle industry had begun to attract the attention of foreign investors.

In 1882, Alexander Hamilton Swan, rancher, cattleman, and businessman from Cheyenne, Wyoming Territory, and Chicago, Illinois, arrived in Edinburgh, Scotland, carrying powers of attorney to represent three Wyoming cattle companies. The Swan enterprise had begun in the 1870's on the windswept Laramie plains of Wyoming Territory. Swan was seeking a buyer who could consolidate his holdings, and the Scots were seeking investments. It was an opportune time for both western cattle and Scottish capital.

For the next sixty years the Laramie plains would bring fortune and misfortune to the Scottish owners. It was the first decade, however, that brought them the greatest ill-fortune, for after their initial contact with the conditions of the western range-cattle business, the survivors began to acclimatize to the plains. This is not to say that they became "westerners," for in truth the West as they envisioned it was already doomed. The West, and the cattle industry, had begun to settle down as a business.

The Edinburgh investors spent fifteen years building and promoting an earlier industry before they realized that the open range was gone and that cattle raising demanded money, management, and detailed attention. The cattle business was no longer a means to sudden wealth or an adventure in nature.

The western range-cattle industry was confronted with many problems, some great, some small. There were two major questions that the industry had to answer: What could they do with the land, and what was the most efficient business structure to promote the industry? The very size of such corporations, however, created other problems. Fencing, range rights, overstocking, and nesters were problems that were aggravated by the great land and cattle companies, whether foreign or domestic.

Many cattlemen sought to meet the needs of their frontier in the 1880's through the collective activity of the cattlemen's associations. The limited-liability company, with absentee ownership, foreign capital, and international politics, was an effective alternative. Both ardent nationalism and international understanding were, from time to time, stimulated by the advent of the British into the cattle industry of the western plains.

The Swan Land and Cattle Company is a case study of these phenomena. It appeared that Alexander Swan, like other cattlemen, had already found the answer to the first question, the use of the land—cattle. Swan's early activity, the formation of Swan Brothers and other companies, and the quest for more capital and greater expansion seemed to provide an answer to the second question. Thus an account of the purpose, the rise and fall, the profit and loss, and the final settlement of the Swan Land and Cattle Company may provide insight into the effectiveness of the cattle company in the development of western economics. How the company affected the other problems on the plains can be seen in its participation in local affairs in Wyoming, its relations with nesters and sheepmen, and its use of fences and public lands.

But the Swan Company was more than just cattle, land, fences, and feuds. It was also men. Of the Americans who were associated with the company, three names stand out as standard-bearers of their time. First and foremost was Alexander Hamilton Swan, the founder and first manager of the company. John Clay, who succeeded Swan as manager and later served on the American executive committee of the company, was one of the best-known stockmen of the West. Curtis Templin, who was appointed manager of the company in 1915, served it and the livestock industry with distinction for the next thirty-five years. In Scotland a long series of distinguished men sat on the board of directors. It would be difficult to single out every individual who contributed to the success of the company, but any such list would have to include the first chairman, Colin J. Mackenzie, and the capable James C. Johnston, who served as chairman from 1916 until 1926, when the company became an American corporation.

HARMON ROSS MOTHERSHEAD

Maryville, Missouri
January 15, 1971

ACKNOWLEDGMENTS

A NUMBER OF persons have been of particular help in this study. First of all, I thank my wife, Ellen, who typed and proofread the manuscript and gave me her unselfish support and her unwavering confidence. Mrs. Enid Thompson, librarian, and Mrs. Kathleen Pierson, of the photographic section of the State Historical Society of Colorado, were of great help in the early research, as was Mrs. Katherine Halverson, chief of historical research and publications in the Wyoming State Archives and Historical Department. My thanks also go to Professors Robert G. Athearn and Clifford P. Westermeier, of the University of Colorado. I owe a particular note of gratitude to John Harr, chairman of the History Department of Northwest Missouri State College, for his sage advice and discriminating comments, and to Dwain Small, dean of faculties at Northwest Missouri State College, for his able assistance in the details of publication.

The photographs included in the book are reprinted through the courtesy of the Western Range Cattle Industries Study, State Historical Society of Colorado.

CONTENTS

Preface   *Page* *vii*

Acknowledgments   *xiii*

Chapter   I.   The Cattle Industry on the
                Western Plains   3

          II.   Founding the Swan Land and
                Cattle Company, Ltd.   19

         III.   Alexander Hamilton Swan—
                A Wyoming Cattle King   44

          IV.   A Year of Disaster   60

           V.   Reorganization at Home and Abroad   84

          VI.   Land and Sheep   112

         VII.   The New Swan Company   142

        VIII.   Conclusion   160

                Appendices   173

                A.   Officers of Swan Land and
                     Cattle Company, Ltd.   175

B. Swan's Business Ventures,
1880–90   177

C. Abstract of Lands of Swan
Land and Cattle Company, Ltd.   180

D. Dividends Paid on Ordinary Shares,
Swan Land and Cattle
Company, Ltd.   182

E. Dividends Paid on Stock, 1926,
Swan Company of Delaware   184

F. Livestock Inventory, Swan Land
and Cattle Company Records   186

G. Ranches Owned by the Swan
Land and Cattle Company   189

Bibliography   190

Index   199

ILLUS

Alexander Hamilton Swan
The Chug Store and Hotel
The manager's complex at Ch
The headquarters at Chugwa
The Hi Kelly Ranch at Chugv
Ranch on the Chugwater, two
The M Bar Ranch house
The Bard Ranch house
Box Elder Canyon
A branch of Sybille Creek
A traction engine breaking sod
Shearing Pens Ranch at shearir
View of Shearing Pens
The bed grounds behind Sheari
Roping a steer to inspect the bra
Branding a maverick
Roundup crew at noon meal
The Swan Land and Cattle Com
"Rounding 'Em Up!"

MAP

The lands and ranges of the Swan Land and
Cattle Company, Ltd., 1884–85   *Pages* 20–21

THE SWAN LAND AND CATTLE COMPANY, LTD.

The Cattle Industry
on the Western Plains

ALONG THE Oregon Trail in the high-plains country of the North Platte there originated, in the 1840's, an industry destined to capture a place in American history far greater than its actual economic value warranted. The open-range cattle industry was a prominent feature of American life for only thirty years, but its impact on the United States has remained a subject of comment and historical research both at home and abroad.

The student of the American West cannot help being amazed by the contrast in the development of the cattle industry in the periods before and after the Civil War. Before the war the attention given to the frontier by politicians and press alike involved the complex and disturbing problem of slavery. The issues of Indians, land, and gold were usually of secondary importance to a nation deeply distressed by the issue of slavery. On the frontier itself, in the mining camps, trappers' tents, and trading posts, the issue of slavery was secondary. But then, the voice of the frontier was often lost in the shouting crowds at the Capitol and in

3

the statehouses. While the nation struggled over the issues of sectionalism and sought a national identity, the cattle industry of the western plains was founded.

Chance and necessity were the parents of the industry. It was by chance that freighters on the trail turned out their footsore oxen in the fall along the valleys of the North Platte, the Green, the Medicine Bow, or the Laramie rivers, believing that they would never survive the winter, only to discover them in the spring fat and sleek and ready for the yoke. The west-bound immigrant along the trail often found his oxen in such poor condition by the time he reached the high country that he was unable to continue without either resting and feeding them or trading them, usually at the rate of two for one. Thus a profitable business was developed along the trail by retired fur traders and mountain men. Several of them accumulated sizable herds and considerable wealth in trading fresh oxen for the wasted creatures that had come over the trail. Ernest Staples Osgood claims:

> The cattle business of the High Plains began as a result of the necessities of the immigrants along the Oregon Trail, and the earliest herds were brought together to meet that demand. The westward trek of thousands to Oregon and California in the two decades before the Civil War stirred into new activity the far-western trading posts, which had languished following the boom period of the fur trade.[1]

The Oregon Trail herds that had been put together by the mountain men were increased by the herds of the traders from towns along the Missouri River who had established businesses in the Mormon settlements. In 1857,

[1] Ernest Staples Osgood, *The Day of the Cattleman*, 9.

following an edict of the church elders ordering gentiles out of Mormon territory, the merchants quickly exchanged their goods for Mormon cattle. These herds were headed toward the high country; it was hoped they would be safer among the Indians than among the Mormons. These herds were again increased when gold was discovered in the Rocky Mountains in 1858. The cattle that took the miners to the gold country were sold or turned loose to graze. Many a prospector found it more profitable and more to his talents to raise beef for the miners than to dig for gold.[2]

At the outbreak of the Civil War the high-plains cattle industry was still only an embryonic business. It yet remained for the plains to be cleared of the Indian and the buffalo before the range was completely open.[3] Also missing was an extended market. On the high plains the cattleman's market was limited to the freighting business, which supplied miners with beef, and some small accommodations for forts and reservations. While the railroad would soon rob the cattleman of his greatest market in the area— freighting—and flood the range with homesteaders, it would at the same time open all the world as his market place.

Throughout the early sixties, freighting to the mining communities and providing beef for their voracious appetites remained the prime function of the cattlemen in the West. The industry was small and dependent, but it was prosperous. It was after Appomattox that the economic opportunities of the western cattle raiser began to "fall into

2 *Ibid.*, 13–18.
3 Edward Everett Dale, *The Range Cattle Industry, 1865–1925*, 15–32. Dale devotes Chapter II of his book to this very problem. The buffaloes were exterminated, leaving the Indian with no choice but to stay on the reservation. The railroad became the new way west.

place like the tumblers of a combination lock."[4] By that time its natural resources had made the West a siren to the opportunist, the speculator, and the gambler. All that was really needed for this exploitation of the West was cheap transportation.[5] In the cattle business of the sixties money was not yet the main problem.

Texas longhorns worth no more than five dollars in Texas could be sold on northern markets for seven to eight times that amount, and there were many Texans who had nothing to do but exchange cattle for cash. The drives began in 1866. Joseph G. McCoy built Abilene, and the rails reached the town in 1867. In the fifteen years after the end of the Civil War nearly four and a quarter million head traveled over the Texas trails.[6] Edward Everett Dale, in *The Range Cattle Industry*, gives perhaps the best account of the northern drive and its effect on the industry. Although there was a need for beef in the North and East and there was a bountiful supply of it in Texas, the railroad made the market possible. The long drives headed north toward the railheads which civilization was rapidly forcing westward. A vision of domesticated herds decimated by Texas fever and crops churned to dust by thousands of cattle moved the Missouri and Kansas farmers to organize resistance to the trespass of Texas longhorns (a practice to be followed later by Colorado and Wyoming cattlemen).

The railroads shipped the fat steers to market and the less finished cattle to cornbelt farms, where they could be

[4] Robert G. Athearn, *High Country Empire*, 128. See also Dale, *The Range Cattle Industry*, xii; and Maurice Frink, W. T. Jackson, and Agnes Wright Spring, *When Grass Was King*, 13.

[5] Athearn, *High Country Empire*, 127.

[6] U.S. Congress, House, *The Range and Ranch Cattle Business*, by Joseph Nimmo, Jr., *House Doc. No. 267*, 48th Cong., 2d Sess., 1888, 28. See also *Tenth Annual Census Statistics of Agriculture* (1880), 975.

fed out and then marketed. Cattle unfit for either destination and those which arrived too late for the market were wintered on the northern plains. This practice proved profitable enough to become a part of the industry, and, as the northern range industry began to grow, it demanded Texas cattle for stocking the range. By the early seventies an estimated sixty to eighty thousand head of stock were grazing within a hundred-mile radius of Cheyenne.[7] After 1875 it became more profitable to sell northern cattle than Texas cattle, and the boom of the late seventies was only a prelude to an even larger boom in the eighties.[8]

By 1870 the trans-Mississippi West had been crossed by the transcontinental railroad, which had become the nerve center of the nation, a system through which the extremities of the frontier ultimately could be reached with ease, comfort, and speed. It was the railroad, reaching hungrily across Kansas, which first introduced Texas beef to the world—and introduced the world to the American West. The railroad was especially responsible for the interest generated in an affluent, investment-seeking Britain. The English and Scots saw, perhaps too quickly and easily, a future and a fortune in western cattle and land.[9]

It was the railroad that made all things possible. By the mid-eighties the buffalo and Indians were gone, the range was being stocked with cattle, the price of beef was high,

[7] Athearn, *High Country Empire,* 136.
[8] Walter Prescott Webb, *The Great Plains,* 232–33.
[9] See W. Turrentine Jackson, *The Enterprising Scot,* for the most recent and authoritative account of British investment. The first five chapters are concerned with the western cattle industry from 1873 to the close of World War II. See also Robert G. Athearn, *Westward the Briton,* for an interesting and lively account of British interest in the American West following the completion of the transcontinental railroad; and Athearn, *High Country Empire,* 130, 141.

land was free (or so it seemed), and profits were estimated as high as three hundred per cent.[10] With all this and a railroad to transport the beef to market, dead or on the hoof, a new bonanza lay before the world. All that remained was the consolidation of the range and the promotion of the business. By the eighties money was a prime necessity, and investors were as eagerly pursuing the cattle industry on the plains as they had pursued gold in the previous decades. "Westward trooped a number of hopeful financiers ready to execute a new exploitation of virgin lands."[11]

Walter Prescott Webb told the story of the cattle boom of 1885. The railroads had crossed the plains and were busily "booming towns" and promoting settlers. An overcrowded East was pushing the farmer with his plow out onto an open range, now free of the Indian menace but fearful of the barbed wire.[12]

If free range, cheap cattle and inexpensive labor were the earmarks of the range-cattle industry of the seventies, money, incorporation, and expansion were those of the eighties. In the seventies money had been available only at ruinous rates, but the cattle industry of that period was such a booming one that it survived and even prospered in the face of the Panic of 1873. Joseph McCoy recalled that at that time over a million and a half dollars in cattle notes were held by the First National Bank of Kansas City and that nearly all were paid off.[13]

The open, unstocked northern plains attracted the attention of cattlemen in the 1870's. For the most part the stock-

[10] Webb, *The Great Plains*, 235.
[11] Athearn, *High Country Empire*, 136.
[12] Webb, *The Great Plains*, 234.
[13] Joseph G. McCoy, *Historic Sketches of the Cattle Trade of the West and Southwest*, 363–67.

ing of the plains required little more than the migration of southern cattle northward. By the early 1880's, however, the ranges were becoming overstocked, and with the arrival of the prairie farmer less and less of the range was open. The range-cattle industry needed money and organization to meet these new challenges. Financial help was sought first at home and then abroad.

Gene Gressley, in his study of the financial aspects of the cattle industry, discovered that easterners invested in the cattle industry for a variety of reasons. Something called "investor fellowship," which originally meant "getting on the band wagon" but turned out to be "misery loves company," was a chief reason for investment. Easterners who were induced to enter the cattle business sought the support and encouragement of their friends and fellow investors. It was the thing to do.[14] Another particularly good source of financing came from those investors who were already putting money in the West, in mining, railroads, and real estate. What most of these investors believed—and rightfully so—was that profit of any great and lasting nature must come from a complete development of the West. So those who already had sunk money in western ventures were inclined to attempt to promote their interests by investing in cattle or in some cases to make a quick dollar to cover slow-return investments. The latter group often involved another, the bankers. Eastern bankers often became involved to protect investments they had already made. Godfrey Snydacker, of the First National Bank of Chicago, is a particular case in point. The Swan Company nearly ruined him.[15] Other backers included meat packers,

[14] Gene M. Gressley, *Bankers and Cattlemen*, 63–68.
[15] *Ibid.*, 66.

such as Nelson Morris; sons of wealthy easterners, the Weares; scientists, such as Louis Agassiz; and many others.[16]

Eastern capitalists and western cattlemen became acquainted in various ways. The publicity of the meat industry and the profit and growth of the cattle industry itself were sufficient to attract many. Southwestern and western congressmen and territorial delegates also did their share. Eastern manufacturers who were in related industries—meat packing and barbed wire manufacturing, for example—were active. Many cattlemen went east to seek backing, among them Mrs. Mabel Day, of Texas, and the Dickey brothers.[17]

The partnership was for a very limited period of time the most popular type of business organization. A cattleman who was already deeply in debt and who wanted to expand and consolidate his operation would form a partnership with an eastern investor. The investor was to supply the money; the cattleman, the management. The split of profit might be fifty-fifty or some other percentage worked out by the two parties. The usual result, however, was that one could tie the hands of the other. "Limited in scope uncomplicated in specifics, the partnership agreement fulfilled the legal requirements of the day."[18] Such partnerships between eastern investor and western manager were frequent but often stormy and dissatisfying to both parties, because "in the shadowy background sat a silent participant—a bank, commission firm or Eastern investors," who refused to become committed or involved in the cattle in-

[16] *Ibid.*, 63–69.
[17] *Ibid.*, 174, 94.
[18] *Ibid.*, 90.

dustry. They saw only good or bad investments and were not builders of empires. Disaster befell many partnerships because the businessman or banker—the silent partner—refused to become more deeply involved in the business.[19] Perhaps the most serious problem of the cattle industry was its size. The West was vast, and there just did not seem to be enough money to fill it. No one could estimate from year to year how much it would take to capitalize the West. "Many a director cursed the day he had subscribed to stock in a cattle company when he discovered that initial capitalization seldom lasted more than the first years."[20]

While the partnership was never very successful, it was a step toward a larger organization—the joint-stock company. From 1880 to the turn of the century, 879 joint-stock cattle companies, both foreign and domestic, were incorporated in Montana, Wyoming, Colorado, and New Mexico, amounting to an aggregate of $284,593,100. Colorado alone accounted for nearly one-third of the number of companies (324) and capital ($102,015,000). Wyoming incorporations numbered only 188, but their total capital amounted to $94,095,800.[21]

Throughout the 1880's and into the 1890's the corporation, or land and cattle company, was the economic livelihood of the cattle industry. As in most other business ventures of the era, the bankers, investors, and commission men, as well as the cattlemen, were primarily interested in making money. Rare indeed was the financier-cattleman, the man who was interested in cattle and ranching and who was willing to reserve profit for improvement and expan-

[19] *Ibid.*, 96.
[20] *Ibid.*, 142.
[21] "Incorporation Records," Western Range Cattle Industry Study (hereafter cited as WRCIS), State Historical Society of Colorado, Denver.

sion. One of the few such men was Isaac Ellwood, of DeKalb, Illinois, a barbed-wire king, who became the largest manufacturer of that item in the United States. He invested in various western enterprises and put 25 per cent of his investment capital into three ranches totaling 246,-247 acres and costing over two million dollars. Ellwood was deeply interested in everything connected with ranching, and his fortune allowed him to indulge in a showplace philosophy. He used nothing but the best, whether building materials or bulls.[22] When one considers how many men were trying to make money out of cattle—everyone from the cattleman himself to the packer and the numerous and sundry middlemen—it is not difficult to realize why more of them lost rather than gained money.

Even during the drought there was as much "watered stock" on the range as there was actual beef:

> A perusal of dozens of ledgers and hundreds of letters between bankers and cattlemen leads to the inescapable conclusion that the Western range cattle industry during the last two decades of the nineteenth century was operated basically on borrowed capital. This dependence is hardly astonishing; as most industrial growth in the Victorian era blossomed on inflated stock issues and borrowed capital.[23]

While various groups in America were busily engaged in exploiting the cattle industry—and one another—others were displaying the attractions of western ranching abroad. Europeans in general, and the British in particular, were interested in the development of the American West. Interest varied according to the conditions of international politics and the financial situation of the European states.[24]

[22] Gressley, *Bankers and Cattlemen*, 78–79.
[23] *Ibid.*, 145.

British capital had flowed to America erratically since the founding of the country. However, it was not until about 1850 that "optimum conditions prevailed" and "English investors, heavily laden with idle capital, were searching for suitable investment fields in the United States."[25] The discovery of gold in California in 1849 attracted considerable capital,[26] but no great amounts were invested until the eve of the Civil War. The war hampered the investment of British pounds, but after the end of the war a greater amount of British capital found its way to the West. It would be difficult to say whether mining or railroads were the greater attraction.[27]

To a large class of people in England living off their investments and therefore constantly seeking new ones, the prospects of the American West were particularly attractive. An insufficient amount of American capital promised high interest rates for foreign investments. "The scarcity of domestic capital pushed interest rates to high levels, which in turn helped draw investments from outside."[28] Americans themselves sought out English capital "for almost every large-scale promotional enterprise either conjured up or initiated in the west."[29]

[24] Clark C. Spence, *British Investment and the American Mining Frontier*, 2.

[25] Frink, Jackson, and Spring, *When Grass Was King*, 135.

[26] *Ibid.*

[27] Spence (*British Investment*, 5) found that "sixty-seven companies were registered with the Board of Trade from 1870 through 1873 to carry on mining and milling in the Trans-Mississippi West exclusive of the Pacific Coast." Turrentine Jackson, in Frink, Jackson, and Spring, *When Grass Was King*, stated that "mining [after 1865] was no longer favored, but investments in the expanding railway network more than replaced them," 135.

[28] Spence, *British Investment*, 8.

[29] O. O. Winther, "The English and the Far West," *The Westerner's Brand Book* (Chicago), October, 1954, 58.

It is not difficult to understand the attraction of British investments to railroads and mining. Both appeared to be profitable ventures. The attraction of the cattle industry was another matter. It was really a combination of an increased demand for beef in England as a result of natural calamities and, at least in the case of the Scots, a nostalgic indulgence in their nation's pastoral past.

Anthrax had decimated the herds in Europe during the 1860's, first on the Continent, where the British had traditionally acquired their beef, then in the Isles, in spite of all the British could do.[30] This occurred just as the States were ending their civil struggle and seeking to recoup or expand their fortunes, both abroad and at home. Britain was hungry for beef, and the cattle industry in the United States was seeking a new market.

> Thus it was that at the same time that America was increasing her livestock production by the founding of scores of new ranches on the vast plains and prairies of the West ... the British were faced with the problem of finding new sources of supply for their meat markets.[31]

In the two decades following the close of the Civil War, British travelers, correspondents, investors, and agriculturalists traveled through the West. The attractions of the western American cattle industry were constantly displayed by the British press. By the late 1870's "it was inevitable that with the peculiar conditions in the livestock market both at home and abroad, the British would turn to cattle ranching as a major enterprise in America."[32]

[30] U.S. Congress, Senate, *Report of the Treasury Cattle Commission on Lung Plague of Cattle or Contagious Pleuro-Pneumonia*, 47th Cong., 1st sess., 1882, *Sen. Ex. Doc. 106. 8.*

[31] Herbert O. Brayer, "The Influence of British Capital of the Western Range Cattle Industry," *Westerner's Brand Book* (Denver), May, 1948, 4.

During the late 1870's and early 1880's the British investment community began an investigation of the future of the American cattle trade and its effect on Great Britain. In 1877, James MacDonald, the agricultural expert of the *Scotsman*, was sent by his newspaper to the United States. He reported no immediate threat to British agriculture, but the profit in the cattle industry described by him further aroused British financial interest. In 1879 the British government sent over a royal commission that reported much the same.[33]

In 1880, W. Baillie Grohman spelled out the prospects and profits in cattle ranching in the United States. He had spent considerable time in the West and was as well acquainted with the area and the industry as any Britisher. He too was impressed by the profit which could be made in the industry, noting that earlier a man had been able to double or quadruple his investment in seven months. This profit had fallen off gradually as money entered the industry and competition increased.[34] To the British investor of 1880 it appeared from all available sources that the cattle industry in the American West was a good investment. Land was virtually free and unlimited. All that was needed was title to the waterfronts that traditionally controlled the grazing. It was the water that was important, not the land. Cattle were cheap in the range country and dear on the market. Labor was cheap, frequently thirty dollars a

[32] *Ibid.*, 5.
[33] Frink, Jackson, and Spring, *When Grass Was King*, 140–42. See also James MacDonald, *Food from the Far West*; and Clare Reed and Albert Pell, "Further Reports of Assistant Commissioners of Agriculture and Fisheries," Royal Commission on Agriculture, 1879–82, WRCIS.
[34] W. Baillie Grohman, "Cattle Ranches in the Far West," *Fortnightly Review*, Vol. XXVII, 438–39.

month for a cowboy who could look after a thousand or more cattle. Under almost any circumstances he could handle this number, and if the range was consolidated and organized, his manpower might increase by 500 per cent. There were, according to most writers, only two great disadvantages to the investor and to the cattle industry. One was the weather.[35] Drought in the Southwest had caused considerable loss, and severe winters on the northern plains were known to have taken a heavy toll in the cattle herds and practically wiped out sheep herds. But losses from the weather, while great in some years, were not over-all disasters. A 5 to 10 per cent reduction in herd numbers was considered sufficient to meet any loss by nature.

The other major disadvantage was the threatened disaster of disease in the nature of pleuropneumonia. This fear had already been expressed by western cattlemen, and an epidemic would run rampant through herds on the open plains. Another unknown factor, but one which apparently caused little concern at the time, was the market. Awareness of this problem would appear in the later 1880's with the organization of the American Beef Trust and attacks by cattlemen on the packinghouse industry, but in 1880–82 the question seemed only a simple one of supply and demand.

By 1882 the beef-hungry and capital-laden British had been convinced, through their home press and the government, that the western cattle industry was the panacea for their problems. The investment public needed to invest its surplus capital because it lived off that capital. The English had the money to buy the beef, and the western plains appeared to be the prime producer of it. All that was really

[35] *Ibid.*, 443–45.

necessary was to place cattle, capital, and consumer into the right relationship, and the needs of all could be met.

The first great venture of the British into the western land and cattle business was the Prairie Cattle Company, Ltd. J. Duncan Smith, managing director of the Scottish-American Mortgage Company, induced a number of Edinburgh capitalists to form a £200,000 joint-stock company for the purpose of buying land along streams in Colorado and New Mexico. Underwood, Clark, and Company of Kansas City was put under contract to manage the American affairs of the company. The firm agreed to work without compensation until the original capital investment had been returned and an annual dividend of 10 per cent had been paid. At the conclusion of that happy event Underwood, Clark, and Company was entitled to three-eighths of all assets of the Prairie Company. Profits for the first two or three years were all that had been expected, and the Prairie Company increased both its holdings and financial structure.[36]

The success of the Prairie Company fostered a whole series of land and cattle companies from 1881 to 1883. On the northern plains of the United States, in the southeastern part of Wyoming Territory, Alexander Swan, his brother, Thomas, and a group of associates began to create a cattle empire. In those prosperous days of unlimited open range and seemingly unlimited expansion and profit, this enterprising group gathered under their control some of the best land in the territory. The Swans had passed through most of the traditional phases of business arrangement. Joseph Frank, James Converse, and Godfrey Snydacker

---

[36] Albert W. Thompson, "The Great Prairie Cattle Company, Ltd.," *Colorado Magazine*, Vol. XXII, No. 2 (1945), 76–83.

were the eastern partners in a western venture with the Swans. Now, by 1882, all were ready to venture abroad for more capital with which to continue the success of local enterprises. Alexander Swan, who had thus far directed the affairs of the various concerns, became the leader in the venture, which ultimately took him to Edinburgh, Scotland. There he gained the favor of prominent capitalists and won their support in the Swan Land and Cattle Company, Ltd.

CHAPTER II

Founding the Swan Land and Cattle Company, Ltd.

WHEN Alexander Hamilton Swan arrived in Edinburgh in the spring of 1883, he represented three companies of which he was a member and which ultimately would be organized into the Swan Land and Cattle Company, Ltd. All three companies had been incorporated in Wyoming: the Swan and Frank Live Stock Company, founded on February 26, 1881, with a capital stock of $648,000 divided into 6,480 shares at $100 each; the National Cattle Company, founded on July 16, 1881, with a capitalization of $550,000 in 5,500 $100 shares; and the Swan, Frank, and Anthony Cattle Company, incorporated on August 1, 1882, at $700,000 with 7,000 $100 shares. The total capitalization of the three companies came to $1,898,000.[1]

The herds and ranches of the original companies were located in Carbon, Albany, and Laramie counties, in the southeast corner of Wyoming Territory. Thomas Lawson, a Scottish agriculturalist, compiled a lengthy and favorable report on the three companies. His report not only

[1] *Registration of Companies*, WRCIS.

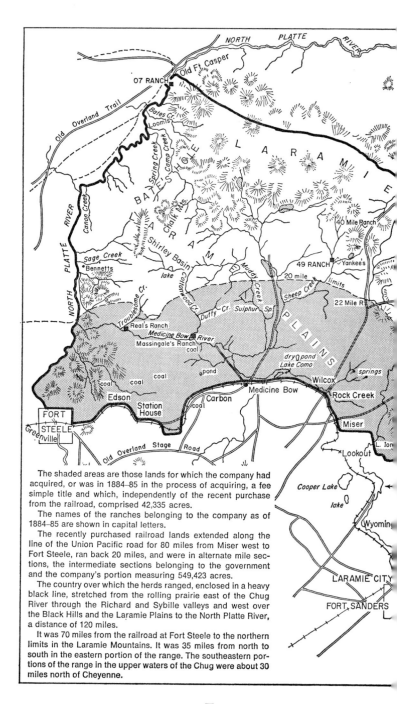

The shaded areas are those lands for which the company had
acquired, or was in 1884–85 in the process of acquiring, a fee
simple title and which, independently of the recent purchase
from the railroad, comprised 42,335 acres.

The names of the ranches belonging to the company as of
1884–85 are shown in capital letters.

The recently purchased railroad lands extended along the
line of the Union Pacific road for 80 miles from Miser west to
Fort Steele, ran back 20 miles, and were in alternate mile sections, the intermediate sections belonging to the government
and the company's portion measuring 549,423 acres.

The country over which the herds ranged, enclosed in a heavy
black line, stretched from the rolling prairie east of the Chug
River through the Richard and Sybille valleys and west over
the Black Hills and the Laramie Plains to the North Platte River,
a distance of 120 miles.

It was 70 miles from the railroad at Fort Steele to the northern
limits in the Laramie Mountains. It was 35 miles from north to
south in the eastern portion of the range. The southeastern portions of the range in the upper waters of the Chug were about 30
miles north of Cheyenne.

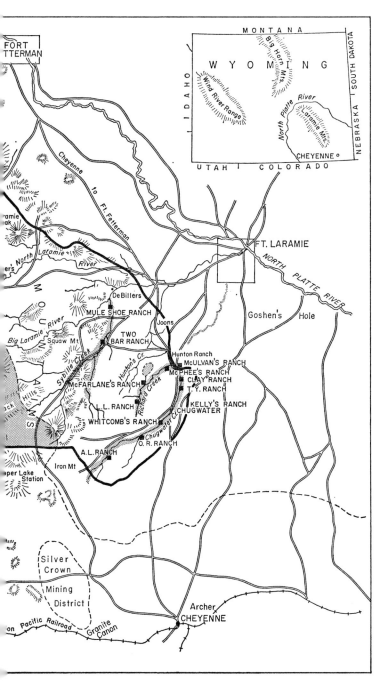

SWAN LAND AND CATTLE COMPANY, LTD., 1884–85

played a significant part in the founding of the Swan Company but also stands as the principal source of information concerning the properties and herds which were purchased. Lawson reported that the ranches formed a "solid block of land about 130 miles long by 42 miles broad at the east end and widening out to about 100 miles at the west end." The Laramie River and the Laramie Peak range formed the northern boundary. The east boundary was determined by the "infall of the Chugwater and top of Box Elder and Cherry Creeks." On the south it was bounded by the headwaters of Bear Creek, and from there "in a westerly course to the Sierra Madre Mountains." The range embraced about 4,500,000 acres of land with scattered improvements. All but about five thousand of an estimated one hundred thousand head of cattle grazing on the range belonged to the three companies.[2]

Nature had blessed the valleys of Chugwater and Sybille creeks with bunch grass, gramas, white sage, and other varieties of grass as rich and abundant as could be found anywhere in America. Nature had also supplied sufficient water. No portion of the range was more than four or five miles from permanent water the year round.[3]

The climate and natural shelter of the country, reported Lawson, drove the cattle to the higher grazing in the summer and preserved the lower grazing for winter, when the grasses cured and formed a winter hay. This left the herds in broken country where they were protected from the severities of the weather. "It seems as if the extreme sum-

2 Thomas Lawson, "Report on the Swan Ranches and Cattle," December 1, 1882. Swan Collection, WRCIS. Hereafter cited as "Lawson Report."
3 Ibid.
4 Ibid.

mer and winter climate of this territory had itself provided natural means for regulating the feeding of the stock."[4] A more ideal place for raising cattle could not have been found. The report concluded: "The Swan range cannot be surpassed in Wyoming either for water, shelter or pasture and I have yet to see any similar extent in that or any other territory as well situated naturally for a combination of all three."[5]

Official sanction of the desirability of Wyoming for ranching came from the pen of Territorial Governor John W. Hoyt:

> Connect with this fact of primary importance that remarkable distribution of water which renders it possible to open innumerable ranches and cattle ranges, which makes almost every square mile of pasturage available; that peculiarity of surface—undulating, with valleys, "draws," canon, bluffs, and hills so distributed and related as to afford to the herds in nearly every locality protection from the storms on the one hand, and on the other secures to them a certainty of food on the ridges made bare (if the storm be snow) by the winds after it is past; that absence of winter rains, so hard upon cattle, so destructive of sheep unhoused; that extraordinary dryness and lightness of our snows which prevent their incrusting and insures their drifting from the ridge and hillocks, so that stock are never long without easy grazing; that no less remarkable dryness of the atmosphere which gives to it the property of a non-conductor of heat and electricity, so that the exposed animals better retain their animal heat and keep their vital forces in full reserve; and last of all, but by no means least, that peculiarity of the autumnal season which cures the rich grasses so gradually and perfectly that all winter long they are as standing hay

[5] *Ibid.*

and even much better (for the ripened seed they retain upon the stock makes them more like grain), associate all these important advantages, unequaled, as I believe, and you have in Wyoming the finest pastoral region in the world.[6]

The governor was perhaps more concise in his views than in his expression of them, but nonetheless he corroborated Lawson's report on the suitability of Wyoming's ranges.

More important to the prospective stockholders than range land were the cattle. Both Lawson and Swan gave detailed accounts of the acquisition, number, type, and grade of cattle. At that time in the range-cattle industry the cost of land, labor, and operation was so infinitesimal that it was of little concern.[7] Cattle were primarily what the company was buying.

According to Lawson, the old stock was "almost all northern and western cattle of good grades." Very few Texas cattle were in the herds. Swan had introduced Hereford bulls in 1878, and nearly half the bulls on the range were either high grades or thoroughbreds. It was estimated that within a year the herd would be raising all the bulls needed for its own use, as well as some for sale.[8]

Swan, in a letter to Colin Mackenzie, chairman of the Scottish company, explained the origin of the herds belonging to the three companies. He and Converse had started with the purchase in March, 1878, of the Searight Brothers' herd of ten thousand, which was discounted at 7 per cent.[9]

[6] Quoted in U.S. Congress, *Report of the Governor of Wyoming to the Secretary of Interior*, November 23, 1885, 49th Cong., 1st sess., 1885, 1181.

[7] Frink, Jackson, and Spring, *When Grass Was King*, 154–57.

[8] "Lawson Report."

[9] The wiser stockmen adopted the practice of deducting certain percentages from the number of cattle carried on the books of the seller. This allowed otherwise unaccountable losses in the herds to be accounted for and compensated for overestimations by herd owners.

This herd, with additions made in the next four years, had been the basis of the National Cattle Company. Of those additions a "few thousand head were discounted at 5% to 10%," and "several thousand [were purchased] by actual count from northwest owners." These, plus the calf brands for 1879–80 and part of 1881, made up the National herd. No deductions were made after that date, but outside branding was not added to the count.

The Swan and Frank Live Stock Company had been formed in February, 1881, with a herd of nineteen thousand owned for the previous two years by Swan Brothers and Frank. It was discounted at 10 per cent. "Most of the additions to the herd during the years 1880, 1881, and 1882 were made by actual count." Before 1880 the herd had been owned by Swan Brothers. "The Swan Frank and Anthony Cattle were all bought during the year 1882 and as soon as purchases were completed the same were formed in August into the Swan Frank & Anthony Cattle Company." When the cattle were not bought by actual count, a 10 per cent deduction was allowed.[10]

The herd books of the three companies contained all sales and purchases to December, 1882. All cattle were classified by numbers of one-, two-, and three-year-old steers; cows three years old or older; heifers one and two years old; and numbers and types of bulls. After 1881 all sales and the names of purchasers were included in the books. Just as important to the prospective buyer was the number of calves branded each year.[11] The combined herds consisted

[10] The above account of the origin of the herds is contained in a lengthy letter from A. H. Swan to Colin Mackenzie, Cheyenne, July 7, 1883, Swan Collection, WRCIS. Special notice is made of deductions since it is of importance in the shortage suit of 1887.

[11] "Original Herd Book" of companies making up Swan Land and Cattle Company, Ltd., 1882 Folder, Swan Collection, WRCIS.

of 87,507 head of cattle, 1,660 bulls, and 833 horses and mules. Nearly half the cattle, 49,032, were of calf-bearing age. Some 15,167 would be marketable steers the following year.[12]

In addition to the cattle and the land, the Scots were also paying for a number of improvements, such as ranch sites, miles of fences, hay meadows, horse pastures, canals, implements and wagons, and all other possessions and rights belonging to the three companies. Like the herds and grazing lands, the remainder of the Swan property was ideal. According to Lawson, "The improvements are decidedly the most permanent and complete I have seen on any ranch in the West and have been planned with judgement and carried out with ability and care." The various headquarters were crossed by a series of irrigation ditches supplying water for extensive hay meadows. These reportedly could be "extended four or five times their present size."[13]

Nearly all the land over which the herds of the Swan companies grazed was open range. Since local cattlemen regarded possession as ownership, they had little fear of being pushed off their ranges. A fence around a tract of land was sufficient to claim possession, and homesteaders were reluctant to move inside such a marker. Pre-emption gave the possessor first opportunity for purchase if the land was placed on the market.[14]

Waterfronts, hay meadows, and irrigation ditches were all secured by titled lands. Lawson recommended, and Swan agreed, that the "balance of the water front" should

---

[12] *Ibid.* See also "Lawson Report."
[13] "Lawson Report."
[14] *Ibid.*

be secured as soon as possible, by "land-script, desert entry, etc., in order to more fully control the range."[15]

Since the possession of the range was apparently determined by the possession of the waterfronts, and since they could be secured permanently only by free title to the land, it seemed desirable that the land titles should be examined. The Scots, relatively ignorant of American land law, employed the law firm of Corlett and Rosedale, of Cheyenne, for this purpose. William Corlett, an eastern-trained lawyer who found health and good fortune in Cheyenne when it was still "on wheels," remained the company's local lawyer for the next several years. Much of the land was unsurveyed or poorly surveyed and title was based on a variety of overlapping and ill-constituted land laws. Corlett's report was therefore impressive in description but necessarily ambiguous in details of law.

There is some disagreement about how Swan and the Scots got together. Swan, in reporting to the first annual meeting, made it quite clear that the sale of the property was not a promotional scheme:

> I may remind you that Mr. Lawson made his report last year on his own authority, and of his own choice. He never was asked to examine or report on the property by my self [*sic*] or any of my associates, but after looking at our ranches and herds, he asked me if they could be put on the market. I said I did not think so, but would see my associates, and if they approved I would be pleased to think over the matter.[16]

---

[15] *Ibid.*

[16] "Report of the First Annual Meeting of the Swan Land and Cattle Company, Limited," April 2, 1884, Swan Collection, WRCIS.

Lawson's role in the Swan affair became one of considerable concern to himself a few years later, when the case against the vendors by the company made him appear to be a party. It was of enough concern to Lawson that he printed and circulated to all the shareholders a letter regarding his role and his opinion of Swan and of Chairman Mackenzie. Lawson was in the business of examining ranch property and notifying parties in Scotland who might be interested,[17] and he had a reputation to protect.

The Scots were confronted with a great array of evidence about the potentiality of the project. With the prospect of a 20 to 30 per cent annual profit[18] and with the further assurance that overproduction was impossible and growth desirable,[19] they found the temptation to buy irresistible.

By the spring of 1883, however, the British press, which had been in large part responsible for promoting the investment of sterling in the American cattle industry, was beginning to urge caution. "One swallow does not make a summer," warned the *Mining World and Engineering Record*, meaning that the apparent success of the Prairie Cattle Company did not guarantee that all similar ventures would be as successful. Some twenty companies had already organized with an aggregate capitalization of four million pounds sterling. The journal was also concerned about why cattlemen wanted to sell if cattle ranching was such a profitable business and why they did not sell to American

---

[17] William M. Pearce, *The Matador Land and Cattle Company*, 3–10.
[18] See Clare Reed and Albert Pell, "Further Reports of Assistant Commissioners," *Royal Commission on Agriculture*, 1879–82, Vol. 71, Swan Collection, WRCIS.
[19] Extracts from "Speech of Sheriff Guthrie Smith, Chairman of the Prairie Cattle Co., Ltd., at the Second Annual Meeting of that Co., at Edinburgh, on 30th December, 1882, Swan Collection, WRCIS.

instead of foreign capitalists. One correspondent suggested that the cattlemen were asking 20 to 50 per cent more than they could get at home. Some properties which had been offered on the market had not proved up to their claims upon examination, and corporate money had had to be returned.[20]

The article continued with special attention to the Swan Company. No proof was offered to qualify Alexander Swan as "one of the most successful and able cattle ranch managers" in America. In place of statistics and facts there existed only a few generalities. The price paid by the new corporation to the original companies was thought excessive. "We shrewdly guess that the profit they will gain for their owners in dying, will exceed those they ever yielded them whilst alive."[21]

In addition to its belief that the Swan Company was based on inflated values and glossy records, the paper also suggested that collusion and fraud were attempted. The author of the article alleged that Lawson's report, from which the prospectus had been written, had been made at the request of Mr. James Wilson, who was to receive six thousand pounds if the deal was completed. The inspection promised by the company before the money was turned over was vague. Was the inspector going to Wyoming or was he also going to stay at his desk in Edinburgh and examine the books, the Lawson report, and similar evidence? The *Mining World and Engineering Record* believed that, in the light of all these practices, the whole matter was

[20] "Cattle Ranch Companies—A Word of Caution," *The Mining World and Engineering Record*, March 24, 1883, 305–306. A favorable reply to the article was to be made the next day. Kerr, Anderson, Muir, and Main to Fraser, March 26, 1883, Swan Collection, WRCIS.

[21] *Ibid.*

"being pushed through with far too much haste, and upon a basis of information which would not be accepted in ordinary commercial pursuits."[22]

A writer in another leading financial journal, the *Scottish Banking and Insurance Magazine*, also added words of caution. Citing the government cases against Swan Brothers for fencing government land and for cutting hay on public land, the writer pointed out the inadequacies of the tenure upon which the land was held. It was further suggested that the weather was more of a problem than most people realized, with severe winters such as that of 1880–81 taking a devastating toll of 25 to 30 per cent of the cattle and wiping out whole herds of sheep. Book count was another major hazard: "It will readily be perceived that this method of innumeration by means of the stock-book is all in favor of the vendor, and most disastrous to the buyer, more especially when no distinction has been made for death rate and strayed cattle."[23] The *London Times* carried a similar article on March 23, 1883.[24]

Before he became secretary of the company, Finlay Dun replied to these fears. He enumerated the dangers that must be considered when buying a cattle ranch and explained how to avoid them. He believed that, since book counts were usually about 25 per cent over herd strength, a purchaser should pay 25 per cent less or reduce the herd by that amount. He held that grazing privileges should not

[22] *Ibid.*
[23] "Cattle Ranching and Cattle Companies," David Marshall to the editor, *The Scottish Banking and Insurance Magazine*, 80, Swan Collection, WRCIS.
[24] See *London Times*, March 20, 23, 24, 1883, for correspondence both condemning and defending cattle and land investments, Swan Collection, WRCIS.

be paid for or that, at the very most, only a nominal fee should be paid for them. Everything else could be easily catalogued and assessed. There should be, according to Dun, small opportunity for difficulty or complication. By dealing directly with the owner, "the real and fancied pitfall" which some correspondents displayed could be avoided. The vendor should become a part of the corporation. He concluded that,

> with the exercise of reasonable care, there is no difficulty at present in buying American cattle and ranches at figures which will yield remunerative returns, . . . there is less difficulty in satisfactorily purchasing a cattle ranch than in securing its continued honest, intelligent, and practical management.[25]

According to the *Prospectus of the Swan Land and Cattle Company, Limited*, the company was "formed to acquire the well-known cattle Herds and Ranches" belonging to the Swan group. Swan, the "successful and able" ranch manager, had paid "special attention to improving the breed of his cattle" and making improvements which were "calculated at once to benefit the herd and increase the control of grazing grounds." The new company, The Swan Land and Cattle Company, Ltd., was being formed to provide "sufficient capital . . . to extend improvements and develop the herds which, combined," would form one of the largest, and best graded herds on the plains.[26] Although the press urged caution and the prospectus left more to faith than to fact, the usually conservative and

[25] Finlay Dun to the editor, *London Times*, March 28, 1883, Swan Collection, WRCIS.

[26] *Prospectus of the Swan Land and Cattle Company, Limited*, 1883, Swan Collection, WRCIS.

cautious Scots quickly raised the capital necessary to found the new company.

In the previous fall the three original companies had made an agreement with James Wilson, of Edinburgh, by which their holdings were to be transferred to a new company by February 14, 1883, provided that such a company could be formed for that purpose. Alexander Swan held powers of attorney to act for the three companies.[27] He himself went to Scotland that winter to help promote the company, and he and Wilson were apparently successful in getting enough interest to conclude the bargain—with conditions. For one thing the powers of attorney held by Swan did not for some technical reason (apparently being too unrestricted) meet the legal scrutiny of the Edinburgh solicitors. Swan returned to the States to meet with the trustees of the Swan and Frank Live Stock Company on December 15, 1882. With Swan presiding they read into their minutes, which were duly notarized, provisions empowering Swan to act for them. According to the minutes, the trustees agreed to sell all property, real and personal, for $983,025 on or about February 14, 1883, as by the agreement entered into with James Wilson of Edinburgh on November 27, 1882, the purchase money to be paid in three equal shares within ten, forty, and seventy days after February 14, 1883. The other two companies soon followed the same procedure.[28]

The promoters themselves were concerned with the book

[27] "Minutes of Meeting of the Board of Trustees of the Swan and Frank Livestock Company," Chicago, December 15, 1882, Swan Collection, WRCIS.
[28] "Notarized Copies of the Minutes of the Three Respective Companies," Chicago, December 5, 1882, January 13, 1883 (two), Swan Collection, WRCIS.

count, control of the company's affairs in the States, the calf brand, and various guarantees that would have an immediate effect on profit. William Stuart Fraser, the Swan Company's Edinburgh solicitor and acting secretary, believed that large investors would be concerned about the purchase of the cattle by book count alone. Recognizing that counting was impossible, an alternative was offered. Swan had suggested a 40 per cent calf brand as reasonable; therefore, if in 1883, or even 1884, the 40 per cent, or 17,868 calves, was not reached, the company would deduct $2,500 for each forty head short.[29] This would not have been much of an inducement to Alexander McNab, a hardheaded Scot, who later became a prominent official of the company. In a postscript to a letter to Fraser he said:

> I enclose report of the Matador Land & Cattle Company from which you will see that their produce of calves is nearly 80 per cent of cows, therefore let Mr. Swan see it if you can and let him understand how much he has to do to come up to that.[30]

That doughty Scot would perhaps have driven even a harder bargain, but which one would have profited is problematic if Swan's note to Fraser is any indication:

> Mr. Anderson when here said that MacNab made the remark that he would double his application if he could be assured of getting good returns regularly. I will give him a written Guarantee sufficient for the case. Making it good for 5 years to give in 8% on Pd stock—if I can have surplus—

[29] Fraser to Promoters of the Swan Land and Cattle Company, Ltd., February 24, 1883, Swan Collection, WRCIS.

[30] Postscript of letter from Alexander McNab to Fraser, April 5, 1883, Edinburgh, Swan Collection, WRCIS.

over that and leave the gain by increased value of herd for him.[31]

Another prospective shareholder was concerned about "the supervision of Marketing & Cash transactions in America." Would they be controlled by the directors, or were they to be left "to the uncontrolled manipulation of the resident manager?"[32]

To allay some of the fears, the prospectus, as already mentioned, called for an inspection of these properties. As early as February, Fraser, secretary and solicitor, began drawing up instructions for the inspector. While not yet specific, the report of the inspector was to include all property, land, cattle, improvements, book accounts, and titles.[33]

All conditions between the parties having been met, the Swan Land and Cattle Company, Ltd., was organized under the companies acts of 1862 to 1880, on March 13, 1883, at Edinburgh, Scotland.[34] The agreement of association was made between Alexander H. Swan, as legal representative of the three companies—Swan and Frank Live Stock Company, the National Cattle Company, and the Swan, Frank, and Anthony Cattle Company, all incorporated under the laws of Wyoming Territory—and James Wilson, of Edinburgh, Scotland, on "behalf of himself and others to be associated with him."[35]

[31] A. H. Swan to Fraser, March 24, 1883, Swan Collection, WRCIS.

[32] William Owens to Fraser, Springdale, Scotland, March 22, 1883, Swan Collection, WRCIS.

[33] Fraser, "Notes for Minute," February 22, 1883, Swan Collection, WRCIS.

[34] The 1862 act was the basic act allowing any seven associates whose object was lawful to constitute themselves a company, with either limited or unlimited liability by means of a memorandum of association. J. H. Clapham, *An Economic History of Modern Britain*, II, 137.

[35] "Memorandum and Articles of Association of the Swan Land and Cattle Company, Limited," March 30, 1883, Swan Collection, WRCIS.

The agreement between Swan and Wilson was the same as that of the previous November, with two amendments. By a supplementary agreement on February 13, 1883, Swan agreed to extend the time for the formation of a new company from February 14 to March 14, 1883. An additional agreement was entered into on March 9 by which, among other things, the parties were to use the prospectus and the "Memorandum and Articles of Association" as the basis for forming the company; the payment was to be made in four equal installments, with interest on the last two, and Swan was to be retained as manager in America, at a salary of ten thousand dollars annually for five years.[36]

The purpose of the organization was to "take over the purchase of and to acquire the Herds, Ranches and others" of the three Swan companies; "to buy, breed, graze and sell cattle, sheep, hogs, horses, mules, and other livestock," or to deal in any related profession or product (such as manufacturing, transportation, and processing); to acquire by various means additional property in the United States of America and elsewhere; to raise and borrow money by means of stocks, bonds, debentures, mortgages, and conveyances in both the United Kingdom and the United States; to carry on financial activity in the name of the company; to buy or merge with any similar company or to sell out to such a company or individual, and "to do all matters of things whatsoever incidental or conducive to any of the aforesaid objects."[37]

The Swan Land and Cattle Company, Ltd., was original-

[36] "Additional Agreement Between Alexander H. Swan, Attorney for the Swan & Frank Live Stock Company and others and James Wilson," March 9, 1883, Swan Collection, WRCIS.

[37] "Memorandum and Articles of Association," Swan Collection, WRCIS.

ly capitalized at £600,000,[38] divided into 60,000 shares of £10 each. Additional capital could be raised by creating new shares upon resolution at special meetings. Increased capitalization occurred in April of 1884 by the creation of 15,000 new shares at £10 each (£750,000), and again in March, 1886, by 15,000 preference shares of £10 each (£900,000). The company could raise the difference between its paid call on the shares and the total capitalization by bonds, debentures, mortgages, conveyances, and similar deeds of security. Most debentures of the company were 6 per cent, and so any dividend on the shares in excess of 6 per cent was profit made on the unpaid capital by the shareholder. As a result of heavy losses in cattle during the preceding years, capital was reduced in May, 1892, to £300,000, with 75,000 ordinary shares of £2 each and 15,000 preference shares of £10 each. Capital was again increased in February, 1898, to £400,000, by the creation of 10,000 5 per cent cumulative preference shares of £10 each. Almost immediately, in May, 1898, the company reduced its capitalization to £250,000. No further change was made until the end of 1917, when capital was reduced to £150,000, and again, shortly before the transfer of the company to an American board, to £7,500. The company conducted its business at general meetings held once a year to present the profit-and-loss statements and carry on general business, and at extraordinary meetings where all other business (such as raising new capital) was conducted.[39]

A board of directors, five to nine in number, originally held five hundred shares each. The number of shares was

[38] The legal rate of exchange was $4.85 to the pound in most cases. In regard to shares it was legally established by the company as $5.00.

[39] "Memorandum and Articles of Association," Swan Collection, WRCIS.

cut in half, however, at the annual general meeting April 2, 1884, when the number of directors was set at eight. In 1918, the number of directors was limited to not less than three or more than seven.

Of the original board members, the chairman, Colin J. Mackenzie, was a landed proprietor and director of the British Linen Company Bank; the others were a manufacturer, the director of Nobel's Explosive Company, a member of the House of Lords, a merchant, a chartered accountant, and a solicitor. The British Linen Company Bank was selected as the company's financial agent; the firm of Howden and Molleson, as accountants; and Fraser, Stodart and Ballingall, as solicitors. Finlay Dun was employed as secretary. Alexander H. Swan was named the manager in America and a member of the board. The brokerage firms of Bell, Beggs, and Cowan, in Edinburgh, and Kerr, Anderson, Muir, and Main, in Glasgow, completed the official directory of the company in 1883.[40]

A significant part of the agreement was the acceptance of some 10,500 shares by the vendors. Amasa R. Converse, Charles E. Anthony, and Godfrey Snydacker accepted them as trustees of the three original companies, and between January and March, 1884, all 10,500 shares were transferred to American shareholders. Converse held 2,517 shares; Snydacker and three members of his family, 2,569; and Joseph Frank, 2,287. A. H. Swan made application for 10,000 shares in his own name. Of these he renounced a total of 5,200, with all but 500 (the latter to John A. Donnelly, of Chicago) accepted by Scotsmen who became major shareholders in the company.[41] Accordingly, Swan's

[40] *Ibid.* See Appendix A.
[41] "Abstracts from Allotment of Shares and Stock Registers 1883–1887,"

original registered holding was 4,800 shares. By April, 1887, Joseph Frank held 3,891 personally and another 1,942 in trust, making him the largest American shareholder, with 5,813 shares. Of the original 10,500 shares to the vendors, 8,626 were still in the hands of American shareholders in 1887.[42] Of the 4,800 Swan shares Joseph Frank bought 2,484 and C. E. Anthony 1,000.[43]

Since one of the stated purposes of the company was to continue the consolidation and improvement of the herds and ranches, the new firm immediately began a study of those conditions. George Prentice, whom the company sent to approve the purchased property, with an eye to the future as well as the present, traveled over much of the Middle West and West—Virginia, Missouri, Kansas, New Mexico, and Colorado. Range conditions on the plains were bad, and roundups were late. During the last week of May, 1883, severe snows and frost occurred over much of Colorado.[44] Swan had also reported heavy snow storms in late April, although the "interest[s] of the company were looking well" and the cattle had wintered in good shape. The roundup preparations were completed by mid-May but obviously did not progress as desired.[45]

At its general meeting in July the company received the Prentice report and his approval of the transaction, in which he declared, "Since visiting the ranges I have again read

---

Swan Collection, WRCIS. Swan used the stock of the company as collateral for other business ventures. When it appeared that he could make an immediate profit on the sale of part of the stock and at the same time relieve some of his indebtedness, he took the opportunity to do so.

[42] *Ibid.*

[43] *Ibid.*

[44] Prentice to Fraser, June 1, 1883, Swan Collection, WRCIS.

[45] Swan to Fraser, May 17, 1883, Swan Collection, WRCIS.

over Mr. Lawson's report, and beg to say that I cannot do otherwise than generally corroborate what he has said."[46]

The chairman of the board, Colin J. Mackenzie, who had joined Prentice on his inspection of the Wyoming ranches, also submitted his report. His report, however, dealt more with the future of the company and therefore consisted primarily of recommendations.

Mackenzie's examination of the Swan range revealed a number of herds, ranches, and lands held by other parties which the company would have to absorb in order to consolidate its holdings. For example, Mackenzie recommended the acquisition of six interests along the Chugwater. Among them was the Clay ranch, two hundred acres of titled land plus improvements, which was owned by Swan, Anthony, and Thomason and could be purchased for five thousand dollars. The Rehmeyer ranch, which the Swan Brothers had acquired for forty-five hundred dollars plus five hundred dollars for hay, was for sale at cost plus six per cent per annum from December 23, 1882. The ranches of Hi Kelly and Colonel Whitcomb were the most desirable and necessary of the holdings to be acquired. Kelly's improvements were some of the best in the country, while Whitcomb's were practically worthless, but together they controlled important waterfrontage amounting to some four thousand acres of titled lands, eighty thousand acres of government land, which they had fenced, and about sixteen hundred head of high-grade and thoroughbred Herefords and Shorthorns.

Kelly, acting for both himself and Whitcomb, was already bargaining with Swan for the sale of the properties.

[46] "Swan Land and Cattle Company, Limited, First General Meeting," July 30, 1883, Swan Collection, WRCIS.

The $450,000 Kelly and Whitcomb had originally asked for their properties had been reduced to $380,000 by A. H. Swan before Mackenzie left Wyoming. This was substantially below the $401,000 evaluation that Mackenzie gave the properties in his report.[47]

The herds and ranches of the Standard Cattle Company, which lay beyond the Whitcomb property and consisted of 480 acres of titled lands and some 8,700 head of cattle, were estimated by Mackenzie to be worth $304,070, while Swan thought they could be bought for $200,000.[48]

The acquisition of these properties would give the company control of most of the desirable lands along the Chugwater and the Richard. The Nagel herd (the Muleshoe Ranch) would give them control of the Sybille. The value of this property, consisting of about one thousand acres of meadow land, some eight thousand head of cattle, and two hundred horses, was estimated at $280,000.[49] Mackenzie proposed that the company "acquire everyone of these properties, even at considerable sacrifice, if that should be necessary."[50]

Like the veins in a leaf, the company's ranches were spread along the Chugwater, the Richard, and the Sybille. While the diversity of holdings gave them greater control of waterfronts and meadows, it also made communication between ranches difficult, since headquarters was at Cheyenne, some thirty-five miles away. At considerable expense to the company Swan and Mackenzie took it upon them-

[47] Colin J. Mackenzie, "The Swan Land and Cattle Company, Limited, Report to the Directors by the Chairman," August 3, 1883, Swan Collection, WRCIS.
[48] Ibid.
[49] Ibid.
[50] Ibid.

selves to install about fifty-two miles of telephone lines, connecting Cheyenne to the headquarters ranch, Hi Kelly's. At a cost of about £1,000, plus £38 annual rent on the instruments, the various ranches were connected with one another and Cheyenne.[51] These purchases and improvements gave the Swan Company uninterrupted control of large blocks of land along the creeks and allowed them to take down fences that prevented cattle from drifting with the storms and secure valuable waterfronts for the company.

On the Laramie Plains, Swan had offered the Union Pacific twenty-five cents an acre on some of its lands. Unable to purchase land at this price, Swan had begun negotiating for a lease with the railroad. Leasing of the land was offered by the railroad at $5.00 a section a year, but the company bargained for $3.20. So that no possibility could be overlooked, Swan took a surveyor to the plains to file on any desirable lands in the alternate government sections.[52]

In the fall of 1883 the desire of Mackenzie and Swan was to secure control over the areas fed by the Chugwater, Richard, and Sybille creeks, and over about 1 million acres of Union Pacific lands on the Laramie Plains, amounting altogether to 3.25 million acres of land. These were to be tied together by a telephone network, connected to one office in Cheyenne where the company had purchased two lots, one for a hotel, the other for a stable, to be used by its men when in town. The range was primarily under the care of two foremen, Al Bowie and Rufus Rhodes. The following year the former was to become head foreman.

Expansion of its holdings and consolidation of the ranges were only part of the concern of the company in 1883. Of

[51] *Ibid.*
[52] *Ibid.*

greater importance were the cattle. Expansion and consolidation meant a greater outlay of capital, with the hope that
the cost could be redeemed in more efficient operation of
the range and sale of the land if necessary. It was the Swan
Land and Cattle Company, and, although most were of the
opinion that cattle meant money, they still looked for every
opportunity to sell land to homesteaders, for town sites,
roads, irrigation projects, and all other ventures from which
they could derive a profit, either from the sale or the increased value of land.

The major concern of all lay in the herds, because immediate dividends could be derived only from the sale of cattle. In March, 1883, Swan compiled for the benefit of the
company an "estimate of the position, increase and profits"
of the company for the next eight years. According to his
projection, the gross growth of cattle would advance from
107,035 in 1883, to 188,675 by 1890, while the net gain
would be from 96,935 to 169,195 for the same time. Total
sales would go from $404,000 the first year to $779,000 the
eighth year, while net profit would increase from an annual profit of $334,417 in 1883 to $675,775 in 1890. Profits
for dividends would average about 16 per cent a year on the
$3,000,000 capital for a total of $3,889,084; herds would increase in the value of $2,108,650, or about 8.75 per cent a
year, while land would increase only about $50,000, or 0.25
per cent a year.[53]

According to Swan's estimates, the cattle would provide
sufficient profit for the future of the company. Any estimate
of the future land values would have been even more
problematic than that of cattle. The years 1882 and 1883

[53] A. H. Swan, "Estimates of Increase in Herds and Profits to 1890,"
March 9, 1883, Swan Collection, WRCIS.

were boom years on the western ranges. The financial possibilities in America and the excess capital in Great Britain made British capital and western beef an ideal combination.

Alexander H. Swan already had three cattle and land companies, which in 1883 held great promise. However, the shrewd Scots were not about to invest large amounts in American companies over which they could have no direct control. In the first place, it would have been poor business. Second, they were unsure about the future of aliens' land rights, of the whole public land system itself, and of the law. The Scots hoped to establish a sound business based on all the information they could gather. Once having secured what they hoped were the proper controls, they entered the fray with a gleam of profit in their eyes.

There is no apparent reason to believe that their motive was to aid in the development of the western cattle industry per se. On the contrary, it appeared to be good business, in which profit could come annually from a very large and mobile crop of cattle. While their initial expansion of herds and grazing had supposedly been for efficiency and practical business, they may also have been a bit overawed by the vastness of the American plains waiting to be exploited.

To Swan and his original partners, the founding of the Scottish company meant security, especially from the astronomical interest rates on American capital for cattle. No longer would it be necessary to borrow money under such killing interest rates as those demanded a decade earlier. It offered another kind of security as well—that of collateral for further investment. There can also be no doubt that Swan himself took great pride in a company which carried his name and which gave him an eminence among American stock growers.

CHAPTER III

Alexander Hamilton Swan
—A Wyoming Cattle King

THE ERA following the Civil War was the period of the self-made man. In every industry men rose from the ranks of the unknown to positions of great importance, some by hard work, others by more devious abilities. But all nevertheless were recognized for their talents.

In the cattle industry there were hundreds of "cattle kings," a title which bore both a connotation of greatness and an implication of greed and cunning. Cattle kings were like leaders in any other industry; some were robber barons, some were captains of their industry. In the cattle industry however, most of the so-called cattle kings were at one time or the other subjected to the hard work of handling cattle. Lewis Atherton, in his book *The Cattle Kings*, describes the rise and fall of most of the major figures in the business. The kings of the industry represent a whole kaleidoscope of personalities, but one thing they all had in common was a penchant to get ahead. They were ambitious men, not of the same breed as the ordinary cowboy. While cattle kings might be considered either captains of industry or robber barons, they, like all other businessmen of the period, had faith in their future and an unbounded opportunity to succeed in whatever they chose, if they had the talents. Without these leaders the network of railroads which spanned the nation, or the teeming factories which manufactured goods at an unprecedented rate, might never have come into being. Alexander H. Swan is such a figure in the cattle industry.

There is something almost majestic about the name Alexander Hamilton Swan. On the one hand, the name suggests preference and a talent for business; on the other, it connotes grace and serenity. The name alone is one that should inspire warmth and confidence. Apparently this is the kind of man Swan was, and it is to him that much of the history of the company must be directed.

In the legendary cattle industry of Wyoming, Swan's career was not the brightest light when compared with those of such men as Thomas Sturgis and Francis E. Warren. Swan's career, however, was more intimately linked to the time and place of the range-cattle industry than that of any of his contemporaries. The dates of Swan's active career in the West were nearly identical to the heyday of the range-cattle industry of the area. He arrived in Wyoming in 1873, and, in partnership with his brother, he rapidly developed a cattle and land business that reached its zenith about 1883–85 and had disappeared by 1887. These dates are identical to the open-range cattle industry of the high plains. The other great names in Wyoming did not achieve their glory in the open-range days, but rather in the consolidating and organizing periods following the disasters of 1886. Swan's career with the Swan Land and Cattle Company was as brief as it was important, and without the record he left behind, the story of the company could not be told.

"Alec" Swan was born in Greene County, Pennsylvania, in 1831, one of eight sons of a farmer of Scottish and Welsh ancestry. Little is known about Swan before he reached his majority. Apparently he received advanced academic training and worked on the family farm until his early twenties. The next three or four years were spent in Iowa, after which he returned to Greene County, Pennsylvania, where he married Lizzie Richie in 1858. The couple moved to Knox County, Ohio, where Swan engaged in land and livestock, but in 1862 they moved to Indianola, Iowa, and there he spent the next ten years. The early ventures of Swan appear to have been directed by his brother, Thomas, who was three years his senior and with whom, in 1873, he formed the partnership Swan Brothers.

Iowa in the 1860's apparently did not offer Swan the freedom of opportunity he sought. However, his cattle-feeding and stock-raising ventures brought him into contact with the feeders, stockers, and shippers of the growing Kansas and Colorado cattle industry which developed rapidly after the Civil War. Swan spent most of 1871–72 in cattle business on the plains.[1]

[1] This sketch of Swan's early life is drawn from C. G. Coutant, "Hon Alexander H. Swan," Coutant Collection; Wilkinson, "The Hon Thomas Swan," manuscript in the Wilkinson Collection; a typed copy of an article by Agnes Wright Spring dated November 25, 1959, nominating Alexander H. Swan for the Cowboy Hall of Fame; and a typed copy of "The Rise and Fall of Alec Swan," by Helena Huntington Smith (later published in *The American West*, Vol. IV, No. 3, 21–24). All are in the Wyoming State Archives and Historical Department, Cheyenne. The articles vary on certain details. Coutant gives 1825 as Swan's date of birth; all other sources give 1831. Wilkinson has the Swans arriving in Wyoming in 1874, while all other sources give the date as 1873. Except for these inconsistencies, the stories are very much the same.

The Swan brothers began their adventure in Wyoming in 1874, with the purchase from John Sparks of a herd of cattle on the Chugwater.[2] One early chronicler described the beginning:

> After a consultation at Greeley, Thomas and A. H. Swan bought the Sparks herd for thirty-five thousand dollars and paid down about fifteen thousand dollars it being about all the cash they possessed at that time. The[y] succeeded beyond their expectation and bought two or three more herds the same year.[3]

Operating from their headquarters on the Chugwater, the Swans began to acquire other herds and ranches on that creek and on the Sybille; they struggled to gain control of the area bounded by these two streams.[4]

Seeking additional capital and talent, the firm of Swan Brothers entered into a copartnership with a third brother, Will F., and the father, Henry. With this new partnership Swan's assets were approximately 13,500 head of cattle, with attendant ranch buildings, houses, and other range property; a one-half interest in the Searight herd and ranches; a number of cattle and hogs in Iowa; 720 acres of land in Warren County, Iowa; and seventy-five shares in the First National Bank of Atchison, Kansas. The partnership, which was to last five years unless otherwise dissolved by mutual consent,[5] ended about a year later, when Henry

[2] This is the apparent date. Wilkinson has both of them arriving in 1874, Thomas in April and Alexander in June. Hubert Howe Bancroft (*History of Nevada, Colorado and Wyoming,* 800) has Alexander arriving in 1872 and being joined by Thomas in 1874.

[3] Wilkinson, "The Hon Thomas Swan."

[4] *Ibid.*

[5] "Articles of Copartnership of Swan Brothers," January 8, 1879, photo copy, WRCIS.

retired from the firm.[6] Henry and his son then purchased the Ell-Seven (L7) Ranch, which they operated for several years.[7]

Alexander and Thomas continued with the development of the area through the organization of various cattle and land companies. It appears that while Tom, the older brother, may have dominated the early years in Iowa and Ohio, "Alec" was the leading figure in the western phase. Swan's activities in establishing the herds and ranges which he eventually sold to the Scottish company have already been alluded to, and, although they were of the greatest significance to the company, they do not alone explain Swan's importance.

During the decade of the 1870's, Swan, while laying the foundation for his future empire, was also active in two organizations that were eventually to rule in Wyoming. One was the territorial legislature; the other, the fledgling Wyoming Stock Growers' Association (WSGA). Swan served as chairman of the Laramie County Board of Commissioners in 1877, and was then elected to the territorial legislature, where he served one term.[8] According to the historian C. G. Coutant, Swan had served one term in the Iowa legislature before coming to Wyoming, and he declined a nomination to the territorial legislature the year he arrived.[9] In 1880, Swan was nominated, by what the *Carbon County Journal* (Rawlins) called the "conservative wing" of the Republican party, as its delegate to Con-

---

[6] *Cheyenne Daily Leader*, January 8, 1880.

[7] See Herbert O. Brayer, "The L7 Ranches," *Annals of Wyoming*, Vol. XV (January, 1943), 5–37.

[8] *Cheyenne Daily Leader*, November 13, 1877.

[9] Coutant, "The Hon Alexander H. Swan."

gress.[10] He made no campaign and was defeated by M. E. Post, but by only 141 votes out of the whole territory. One might say that Swan lost by default, and his near win was a testimony to his great popularity and ability.[11] He ended his political career by serving as a delegate to the Territorial Republican Convention of 1882.[12]

During the same period Swan was active in the Wyoming Stock Growers' Association. Swan Brothers was admitted to membership in the association (then the Laramie County Stock Association) on April 5, 1875,[13] and about a year later Alexander Swan was appointed to a committee to work with the county commissioners for the employment of detectives. In the same year he was elected to serve as secretary pro tem, and then he became president of the association.[14] In 1879 he again served as president, after defeating Joseph M. Carey for the post.[15] Swan was a member of a committee in 1883 appointed by the WSGA to negotiate with the railroad interests in Chicago for reduced rates on the shipment of cattle and free transportation for stockmen. At the same time he represented the stockmen at a convention in Illinois, where he sought the support of that state's representatives for legislation to control contagious diseases.[16] The railroad negotiations netted some success.[17]

[10] *Carbon County Journal,* (Rawlins), October 16, 1880.

[11] C. G. Coutant Collection; *Carbon County Journal,* October 23, 1880.

[12] *Carbon County Journal,* September 9, 1882.

[13] "Laramie County Stock Association Minute Book Proceedings," April 5, 1875, Wyoming Stock Growers' Association Collection.

[14] "Laramie County Stock Association General Meeting," March 10, 1879.

[15] "Laramie County Stock Association General Meeting," March 28, 1879.

[16] *Carbon County Journal,* July 7, 1883.

[17] *Ibid.*

After the organization of the Scottish company all was not harmony between Swan and the stockmen's organization. As Swan became more active in the acquisition of cattle and ranches, he became less so in the association and in politics. During the same years Thomas Sturgis, the secretary of the organization, was its reigning figure, and under him it rose to dominance in Wyoming. According to historian W. Turrentine Jackson, for the remainder of the nineteenth century the WSGA was the real power in Wyoming.[18]

Swan and Sturgis headed two different elements in the association. In the words of John Clay, there were "two factions in cattle circles at that time in Cheyenne. A crowd worshipped at the shrine of Swan; another looked to Tom Sturgis for inspiration."[19] Although Clay distinctly states that to those on the inside "the lines of demarcation were plainly marked,"[20] he does not illustrate the reasons. There are bits of evidence about the differences. Swan and his group did business at the First National Bank; the others, at the Stock Growers' Bank.[21] But this in itself cannot explain the factionalism. The better explanation lies in the changed nature, organization, and personnel of the association.

Swan had been president of the association from 1876 to 1881; Sturgis, its secretary from 1876 to 1887. In 1879 the organization changed its name to the Wyoming Stock Growers' Association; it created a full-time executive com-

[18] W. Turrentine Jackson, "The Wyoming Stock Growers' Association, Political Power in Wyoming Territory 1873–1890," *Mississippi Valley Historical Review*, Vol. XXXIII (March, 1947), 571–94.
[19] *Ibid.*
[20] John Clay, *My Life on the Range*, 65.
[21] *Ibid.*

mittee that was to have control of all its activities when it was not in session and to represent the association before the legislature. At the same meeting membership by firms was repudiated and granted to "individuals" only; thus, when two members of a firm wanted to participate in the activities and business of the association, each had to become a member. Since dues were collected from members according to the assessed valuation of the herds, it meant that large companies would be assessed for each member. For these changes in the association Clay gave credit to Sturgis. He was also proclaimed by Clay as, "intellectually, standing head and shoulders above them all."[22]

The year 1884 found the territorial legislature confronted by the WSGA for the passage of a "maverick bill." What the association wanted, and what it got, was for all unbranded animals to be turned over to it; the proceeds from their sale were to be used for inspection and detective services. The bill was strongly opposed by small ranchers and cattlemen alike, as well as by some of the larger firms. They were not opposed to the sale of mavericks, but they preferred the territory to have them. Swan, in particular, was opposed to the bill. Sturgis telegraphed to Swan for an explanation of his opposition and received this reply:

> I never agreed to support the maverick bill. Never read it until after leaving Cheyenne. Am ready to give full support to any measure which will give justice to cattle owners. Do not consider present bill just in its provisions and if passed will be unsatisfactory in results.[23]

Moreton Frewen, however, received a much fuller expla-

---

[22] *Ibid.*
[23] *Ibid.*

nation to a similar inquiry later in the year. From Swan's response it would appear that he had been accused not only of opposing the bill, which he readily admitted, but also of engaging in unethical practices concerning that particular law. This he emphatically denied. He had paid his assessments and calls,[24] he said, and he had not conspired with his foremen to buy mavericks at fifty cents a head, although other parties might have been buying mavericks at such a price. It was not his responsibility to fight the bill as unconstitutional, and he noted that it was "the privilege of those who think it proper and constitutional to enforce the Law and thereby prove its constitutionality."[25] Neither had he received instructions from the Swan Company concerning action on the law. He also feared this bill would not be the last. He considered it "only as a stepping stone to one still more obnoxious which no doubt will be presented at some future time."[26] Swan's intimation was echoed by Finlay Dun in 1887 when he wrote the home office: "Enclosed is a demand from the Wyoming Stock Growers' Association for upwards of £600,—as a contribution—in addition to the cost of mavericks—for which we have paid something like £800, and more than half of them have certainly been our own cattle."[27]

Swan apparently had more faith in the democratic processes, preferring the legislature to the Stock Growers'

[24] The WSGA, in its early days, found it necessary to call for money from its members beyond the amounts acquired by assessments, in order to meet special or emergency needs.

[25] Quoted in Helena Huntington Smith, "The Rise and Fall of Alec Swan," *American West*, Vol. IV, No. 3 (August 1967), 23.

[26] A. H. Swan to Moreton Frewen, August 25, 1884, Swan Collection, WRCIS.

[27] "Report of Finlay Dun in Wyoming June 8 to October 2, 1887," Swan Collection, WRCIS.

Association as the controlling body of the cattle industry, and doubting the justice of a vested interest group for all concerned. If the Johnson County War is taken as proof, his faith may not have been misplaced.

It can be said without doubt that Swan was acquisitive and expansionistic. His interests were in the whole of the West and not alone in cattle and Wyoming. Swan's interests included land, railroad, real estate, cattle, stockyards, banking, and various social and fraternal organizations; they were simply too broad to be governed by a stock growers' association. The attitude of the company reflects that of Swan: "This association does not benefit us much; it is stupidly and wastefully managed; some of its laws and regulations are absurd and unworkable; even if it dies from want of funds it will not be seriously missed."[28]

The Stock Growers' Association had nothing to offer Swan that could not be had from the legislature, and it would, in fact, restrict his activities. Many of the very things adopted as association regulations and/or territorial legislation had already been practiced or suggested by Swan. Upgrading the quality and fecundity of the herds by improving the types and increasing the number of bulls, as well as withholding the bulls from the herds until certain dates to prevent early calf loss owing to late spring storms, are good examples of Swan's foresight. These practices later became range regulations of the association.

Swan and his kind were gamblers, and the association was amazingly regulatory, for both member and nonmember alike. Much of the atmosphere of this period is portrayed in John Clay's *My Life on the Range*. From it one gets the impression that there were really two types of men

[28] *Ibid.*

in the range-cattle industry. The first was the "gambler," the cowman with a small amount of money and a talent for collecting herds and filling a good hand, but more often running the bluff than holding the ace. The other was the banker, who ultimately could always cash in. All the banker needed to do was wait until the gambler was short and then win. Swan was the first type; Sturgis was the latter, as was Clay himself.

Although Swan may have been at odds with the Stock Growers' Association and restricted his activities in that group, he was active in many other concerns. Two of his greatest ventures, other than the Swan Land and Cattle Company, were the Wyoming Hereford Association and the Union Stock Yards in Omaha. Swan appeared to be headed toward vertical organization of the cattle business: breeding, raising, fattening, marketing, transportation, and sales. He does not appear to have been interested in the packinghouse business.

Swan had been active in the purchase and breeding of Herefords for some time. The *Cheyenne Sun* of November 10, 1881, editorialized on the desirability of Herefords, noting that a lot of grade animals shipped from Denver, in 1873 had sold in Buffalo, New York, for about eighty dollars a head. The Swan Brothers had purchased a herd that used thoroughbred Herefords, Shorthorns, and Galloways, the produce of which had led Swan to adopt the Herefords. The *Carbon County Journal* of May 27, 1882, announced the arrival in Chicago of "several carloads of young Hereford bulls" with more to follow. The bulls had been purchased in Illinois, Indiana, and Michigan by Swan Brothers and Frank, and were on their way to Wyoming to be sold among the ranchers to upgrade the quality of their herds.

The same journal, about a year later in an item from the *Drovers Journal* of July 17, 1883, recorded the progress of a large herd of Herefords belonging to Swan Brothers, on its way to Wyoming. The herd, some 225 head of Hereford bulls, cows, heifers, and calves and five polled Angus, was judged to be the "largest and best lot of Hereford cattle that has ever been imported into the United States." The cattle had arrived in Baltimore in April and were held there under quarantine since that time; one prize bull alone had been sold to a Muscatine, Iowa, breeder for one thousand dollars.[29]

Apparently the desirability of Hereford breeding stock had proved itself to the Swans, for in August, 1883, the Wyoming Hereford Association was incorporated in Laramie County, Wyoming Territory. A. H. Swan, Thomas Swan, C. Boulter, C. E. Anthony, and George F. Morgan were the trustees. The capital stock was $500,000 in $100 shares.[30] The new organization combined the two herds mentioned above, making up a herd of about four hundred Hereford bulls and cows, and placed them on a controlled range, the Kingman Ranch, about six miles east of Cheyenne. The company built a one-hundred-stall barn for the finest bulls and open sheds for the rest of the herd. Bulls and cows with calves were fed during the winter; the rest of the herd was fed only when the ground was covered with snow. It was from this herd that the prize Hereford bull Rudolph, valued at ten thousand dollars, came, to win many honors in livestock shows around the country. Swan's initial venture in Herefords remains today in the Wyoming Hereford Ranch.

[29] *Ibid.*
[30] *Carbon County Journal*, July 21, 1883.

In 1883, Alexander Swan founded South Omaha and started the Union Stock Yards in that city. More precisely, Swan persuaded W. A. Paxton of the Transfer Stock Yards in Council Bluffs, Iowa, to transfer his operation to Omaha, and he encouraged a group of Omaha investors to finance the development of the land and the yards. F. W. Lafrentz, in a letter to Russell Thorp in 1946, gave this account of the project:

> Well do I remember our sitting side by side on one of the hand trucks in the Union Pacific Station at Omaha, waiting for the train to come over from Council Bluffs, when he said to me; "I have authorized my brother-in-law Lem [L. M. Anderson] to acquire options on 2000 acres of land South of Omaha, on the river—so be ready to make the payments he will call for." I asked, "What are you going to do with it?" He replied, "I am going to create the town of South Omaha, and will try to get Bill Paxton to move his stock-yards there from Council Bluffs—and then I will try to have the Chicago packing houses build plants there, which will mean that all the railroads will build spurs into town." And he succeeded beyond all expectations.[31]

The South Omaha Land Syndicate was formed August 30, 1883, and included Swan and Paxton as well as Colin J. Mackenzie.[32] Swan was the first president of the syndicate and one of the members of the board of trustees. The syndicate was to establish stockyards and a suburban town for workers in the yards and slaughtering houses. This venture was by far the largest and most profitable engineered by Swan. By 1885 the South Omaha Land Syndicate had

[31] *Cheyenne Sun*, August 11, 1883.
[32] F. W. Lafrentz to Russell Thorp, August 7, 1946, Alexander Swan 2d Collection, Western History Research Center.

an estimated valuation of $11,400,000. In January, 1887, the trustees of the syndicate transferred their property to a third party, John H. Bosler, for $700,000. Bosler, in turn, conveyed the property to the South Omaha Land Company in February, 1887, with a capital of $1,000,000, and Swan became a member of the board of trustees of that company.

Swan negotiated with L. M. Anderson to purchase some 1,300 acres in the South Omaha area. By August, 1883, Anderson had secured 1,875 acres at a cost of $312,972.73, or about $167 an acre.[33] After Anderson had invested $10,000 on the project, A. H. Swan stepped in and raised another $40,000 among Omaha capitalists. With this undertaking the stockyards and South Omaha seemed to be assured.

A second legally distinct company, the Union Stock Yards Company of Omaha, was formed on December 1, 1883. It was organized in Omaha by Alexander H. Swan, William A. Paxton, John A. Creighton, Peter E. Iler, John A. McShane, Thomas Swobe, and Frank Murphy with a capitalization of $1,000,000. The stockyards commenced operation when $700,000 had been subscribed. The Union Stock Yards Company had been organized for the "purchase and sale, the feeding and caring for, slaughtering, dressing, packing and holding for sale, selling, and selling for others, of livestock."[34] The company organized immediately, with Paxton as president and Swan as vice-president. All the incorporators served on the board of directors, and Swan became president the next year.

The year 1883 appeared to be a banner year for Alexander Swan. Most men would have been content with the

[33] This account of the founding of the stockyards and South Omaha is from James W. Savage and John T. Bell, *City of Omaha Nebraska and South Omaha*, 593–600, 613–20.

[34] *Ibid.*

creation, in a single year, of any one of these companies. Swan had in one year founded companies with a total capitalization of $5,700,000, all of which materialized and prospered for a period of years. Swan was not, however, content with these projects, for on November 10, 1883, the Cheyenne, Black Hills, Montana Railroad filed incorporation papers for a company capitalized at $10,000,000.[35] Earlier in the year, on May 16, Swan and others had incorporated the Union Mercantile Company for $20,000 to carry on general merchandising business in Cheyenne.[36] These two companies would bring the figure for the year 1883 to some $15,000,000, a really astonishing accomplishment for a man who only ten years before had, with his brother, started in the Wyoming cattle business with $15,000.

Alexander H. Swan is without peer in the early days of the cattle industry of Wyoming. It is difficult to find anyone quite like him among all the other cattle kings. He seemed to thrive on success. Each success meant a greater opportunity to succeed, and he never hesitated to open the door to opportunity's knock. There were those who did not like Swan, but they were his competitors and often his rivals. He was an empire builder who owed much of his success to his own personality. Unlike many captains of industry, he did not have troubles with his employees. He does not appear to have been guilty of determined, premeditated fraud. He did not buy up bankrupt ranches and

[35] Savage listed the members of the Syndicate as "A. H. Swan, C. A. Righter, Colin J. Mackenzie, M. C. Keith, August Richard, W. A. Paxton, Milton Rogers, J. E. Markel, Thos. Swobe, John A. McShane, Iler & Co., Caldwell, Hamilton & Co., Frank Murphy, Ben B. Woods, Geo. E. Baker, Samuel E. Rogers, J. M. Woolworth, J. H. Dumont, Charles F. Manderson, Benj. F. Smith, and Samuel Allerton."

[36] *Carbon County Journal*, November 10, 1883.

sell them to unsuspecting stockholders. Swan was interested in the cattle industry, in the raising and breeding of cattle for the benefit of the industry, and not solely interested in making money, regardless of the product or service provided. His business practices were, on the whole, far more ethical than the moral climate of the period demanded.

By 1883, Swan was sitting at the apex of an empire built on cattle and commercial paper. In some sense all his enterprises were related to the cattle industry. But the cattle and the weather were unpredictable; and paper, after all, was only paper, as Swan and many Scotsmen were to discover.

CHAPTER IV

A Year of Disaster

IF THE YEAR 1883 was a banner year for Swan and the cattle industry, 1887 was one of disaster. Honor, pride, and fortune—all were challenged in 1887. Three events of that year, initially unrelated but in many ways inseparable, were the keynotes. The first was the beginning of a suit against Swan and about fifteen of the other vendors for alleged shortages in the original herds. The second was the failure of the firm of Swan Brothers. The third was the devastating winter of 1886–87. It is ironic that Swan's failure occurred in the same season that nearly destroyed the cattle industry in Wyoming and brought an end to the open range. It is equally ironic that the shortage suit against Swan was rendered ineffective when existing evidence was destroyed by the great death toll on the cattle that winter.

The company had increased its capitalization in 1884 in order to buy the herds and ranches of Kelly and Whitcomb. Shortages appeared in the herds when branding began, and, as a result, 7,900 head were written off in 1884 and 3,000 more in 1885. Of the 11,500 Texas steers bought and turned out on the range in 1884, only 480 head could be found in 1885. More cattle were written off in 1886, and the Scottish shareholders began to grumble.

Herd losses had been investigated by Swan in 1885 and he recommended that the company "should write off the same percentage both off the herd and off the bulls and in the same way as was done last year as no doubt it will be better for us to make these annual deductions in order to keep the herd in a solid and substantial condition."[1]

Losses and shortages in the calf brand were laid to a number of causes. A high percentage of cattle judged as barren on the range were discovered to be with calf when slaughtered. Too many cows were sold. The company expected an unreasonably high percentage of calves. The Kelly and Whitcomb herds had returned only a 50 per cent calf crop in both 1883 and 1884 under ideal conditions. Losses from severe winter weather and early spring storms caused a 20 to 25 per cent loss by abortion.

An undetermined number of calves escaped the branding iron during the usual branding seasons. Since they were never tallied, cattlemen chose to believe that the outside calf brands were equal to the losses their herds sustained from bad weather. This was not the case however, in the Swan herds or any other. Swan reported to Finlay Dun that "the average of losses were not made good in that way."[2] Certain classes of cattle were affected more than others by the weather. No sales had been made in 1881–82; "hence any shortage that may now be or hereafter be felt to exist must necessarily arise from the fact that percent-

[1] Swan to Dun, January 1, 1885. (Unless otherwise indicated, all citations in this chapter are from the Swan Files of the WRCIS.)
[2] Swan to Dun, January 8, 1885.

ages sufficient were not allowed or deducted annually."[3]

These recommendations and observations were the result of James Tait's visit to the ranches in July and August of 1883.[4] Tait, one of the directors, had been a critic of Swan's management from the very beginning. He had opposed acceptance of the book count, had constantly argued that the price Swan paid for the additional ranch property and herds in 1884–85 was too high. He was especially critical of the purchase of the Reel herd and ranches, and became the first to agitate for a suit against the vendors for shortages in the original herds. Upon his return to Scotland in 1884 he drafted certain recommendations. He was, he said,

> satisfied that in order to obtain the best results from the business, it is necessary to attach much more importance than has hither to been done to the protection and sheltering in bad weather, as also to the systematic sub-division, classification and separation of cattle.[5]

He therefore recommended that the cattle should be divided into about fifteen convenient-sized herds of some ten thousand each, that there should be a foreman and crew of about twenty men a ranch, and that each herd and ranch should be separated by extensive fencing. Feed, shelter, and barns should be provided for all cattle during bad weather. With proper control of grazing and use of feed the company could finish its own cattle on its own ranges before sending them to market. Slaughterhouses and stockyards might be established in the future whereby the company could ship its own meat to market by refrigerator cars.

[3] *Ibid.*
[4] Swan to Dun, January 1, 1885.
[5] "Notes, James Tait's visit to Ranches," August 22, 1884.

The company, by following these recommendations, could do away with the distillery feeding operation,[6] increase the marketing value of animals from five dollars to twenty dollars, avoid loss by straying, allow for a better accounting of the cattle, and let each ranch operate more independently. Tait knew that the scheme he had proposed was judged impossible by both Swan and Al Bowie, but he cited many small ranches that were doing the very things he recommended.[7]

That Tait and Swan differed on the proper operation of a ranch was obvious; therefore, it was unlikely that Swan was greatly surprised when he received the following letter from Tait, dated March 29, 1886:

> Referring to the conversation I had with you at the close of the meeting of 25th inst. I think it only right to let you know that I intend to propose at next meeting of the Board that claim be made on you and your co-vendors for the value of the 7900 head of cattle admitted by you not to have been in existence at the time of transfer of the three herds to the company. Of the exact terms of the resolution which I propose to submit to the Board you will be duly advised, but it will refer only to the 7900 head of cattle mentioned.[8]

Swan was instructed to inform the other vendors and notify Tait about their decision. This was only a preliminary skirmish to remove Swan.

It was obvious by the spring of 1886 that certain mem-

[6] Following a common practice of cattlemen, Swan had for a period of years contracted with an Omaha distillery to stable and feed unfinished steers on distillery slops. This had been of uneven success and was discontinued when cattle prices dropped and distilleries raised their prices.
[7] "Notes, James Tait's visit to Ranches," August 22, 1884.
[8] James Tait to Swan, March 29, 1886.

bers of the board felt that Swan had mismanaged the company and that the vendors had not met their obligations. Cattle were the main investment of the company, and it appeared that there were shortages. Swan readily admitted this and explained to Dun that deductions in the herd numbers would have to be made because of the severe winters over the past six years and especially the past three. Losses had been greater than the cattlemen had anticipated, and, he agreed, now that they had shown up, some allowance had to be made.

Such were the events that ultimately led the company to institute a case of fraud and misrepresentation against Swan and about fifteen of his associates. Preparation for the suit began as soon as the results of 1886 were known. William Fraser arranged with the Chicago law firm of Swift and Campbell to investigate the possibilities of a case and to institute it, if they felt satisfied that the action was justified. The Chicago attorneys were busy, and although they promised to proceed with the case around the first week of February, it was not until the first of March that they finally sent their preliminary report. They believed that the company had a case. Even though the three original companies had dissolved, the individual members of the companies could still be sued. Since the vendors had guaranteed the correctness of the book count, they were responsible for any loss.[9] The attorneys recommended that Swan should be dismissed to prevent any interference in obtaining evidence in the case.[10] On May 17, 1887, Swift cabled Fraser that the firm of Swan Brothers had failed. On May 21, Fraser cabled Swift that Swan had been sus-

[9] Swift and Campbell to Fraser, January 13, and March 3, 1887.
[10] Swift and Campbell to Fraser, May 5, 1887.

pended from the management of the company and that Secretary Dun was sailing at once to take his place.

It is at this juncture that it becomes difficult to separate the failure of Swan Brothers from the company's case against Swan himself. The two events occurred at the same time. The company, while investigating a suit of fraud against Swan and the other vendors for not having the cattle they claimed to have, also discovered evidence that Swan had turned company money to his own use and that the company in many cases was responsible. In the latter situation there was nothing the company could do but pay the notes and collect from Swan. Swan was already in receivership, however, and there were no assets available except what shares he still held in the Swan Land and Cattle Company.

The details of the failure of the firm of Swan Brothers are relatively brief:

> The direct cause of this suspension is due to the action by attachment brought against A. H. Swan by the German Savings Bank of Davenport, Iowa, on a note which had been signed by Swan as security, and when no ultimate loss could occur because of the bank being fully protected by the property of the principal. . . .

So announced the *Kansas City Livestock Indicator* of May 19, 1887. The paper assured its readers that assets of the firm were in excess of its liabilities. Swan Brothers decided on suspension after $85,000 had been paid out to creditors and it had made an assignment of $1,100,000. Swan had been in Scotland at the time the action was taken, trying to raise backing for a new company, the Iowa Land and Thoroughbred Livestock Association, whose inventory amounted to precisely £85,447.4.2.[11] Swan was carrying bonds for considerable Iowa property, and he wanted to found a new company with Scottish capital to relieve himself of the heavy securities. Banking authorities doubted that Swan Brothers would be able to pay in full, and there was concern in all the cities from Cheyenne to New York where the firm did business.[12]

But there were other causes for Swan's failure:

> A. H. Swan is perhaps the most widely known Western operator among Eastern Capitalists, and to that fact we attribute his present misfortune. Every new and promising business scheme sprung in the entire area of his acquaintance, reaching from New York to the Rocky Mountains was at once submitted to him or a share of his wealth asked in connection with his influence, to put the project on its feet.[13]

Swan had become involved in a number of projects, "some successful and some not," and since he had been the main support, the drain had been heavy. The cattle business was not the cause; real-estate interests were. "The money is all out on real estate," said the *Northwest Live-Stock Journal*.[14] When Swan needed money from the banks for the cattle enterprises, it was not available. His financial structure was so precariously organized that a failure in any one area would have caused a total collapse. Swan Brothers was able to pay only about ten cents on the dollar.

Following the dismissal of Swan as manager, the company sent its secretary, Finlay Dun, to Wyoming to take charge of the ranch. Dun's duties were manifold. He had

[11] *Mr. Swan's Inventory and Report of M. Fisher*, (printed), Des Moines, Iowa, July 22, 1886.
[12] *Kansas City Livestock Indicator*, May 19, 1887.
[13] *Ibid.*, May 26, 1887.
[14] *Ibid.*, item from *Northwest Live-Stock Journal* (Cheyenne).

to determine the exact condition of the company's property and financial condition and to gather evidence of Swan's alleged embezzlement. Land value, titles to lands, improvements, and the number and grade of cattle had to be investigated. The financial assets of the company, the reliability of the men, and the reputation of the company also had to be considered. Dun was to offer suggestions on the management of the company and on its future policy. His success in this venture was of great importance to the company for two reasons: first, it was essential to its case against the vendors; second, it was a necessary foundation for the future policy of the company. In a series of reports by Dun to the home office, and in particular to William Fraser, who was serving as interim secretary, are found some of the most enlightening interpretations available of the conditions of the company and of the character of Alexander Swan.

Swan believed that his suspension and financial problems were the result of the bank attachment on him for the note of Thomas Drimmie, which Swan had signed for security. Swan may very well have had reason for suspicion. Thomas Librum Drimmie was one of the original subscribers to the Missouri Land and Live Stock Company. So also were William Fraser; George D. Ballingall and G. T. Stodart, the members of the Swan Company's law firm; and James Tait, Swan's major critic.[15] Drimmie arrived in the United States in the spring of 1884, apparently interested in land and livestock investments in the Middle West. Very likely he was associated in some way with Thomas Lawson, manager of the Missouri Land and Live Stock Company.[16]

[15] "Memorandum and Articles of Association of the Missouri Land & Live Stock Company, Limited," March 18, 1882.

[16] Urquhart to Fraser, January 3, 1884, February 8, 1884.

Drimmie, "a considerable shareholder" from southern Iowa, supported Swan's managership at the annual meeting in 1886, but it was also his bank note which, a few months later, brought an end to Swan's career in the cattle business.[17] Robert Urquhart, then working in the company's office in Cheyenne, wrote a most interesting letter to Fraser on the relationship of Swan and Drimmie:

> I wonder at Drimmie standing up and saying what he did, as he knows little more about the working of a Ranch more than a cow pony which knows how to turn a steer better than many a cow boy. But I suppose he would think he was called upon to do something to help the old man in respect of his endorsement of a high valuation of his farm to enable him to get a large mortgage on his property. Come light go light I think will be the outcome of Drimmie's money. He puts on too much style around.[18]

Robert Urquhart was a personal friend of William Fraser. He had applied for the position of secretary of the company and had also asked to inspect the company's purchase in Wyoming. Both positions had been given to other people. Through the efforts of Fraser and James Tait he had secured a post in the office of the bookkeeper, Fredrick W. Lafrentz, and he and his wife had moved to Cheyenne sometime in the early spring of 1884. From that time on he became a critic of Swan and a self-appointed informer to the home office on all that occurred in Wyoming.[19]

Urquhart was also a drunkard, which probably explains why he did not receive any of the positions of trust. In his letters to Fraser he complained that in some manner or

[17] "Report of the Third Annual Meeting," March 12, 1886.
[18] Urquhart to Fraser, April 19, 1886.
[19] "Robert Urquhart Reports, 1885–1886."

other Swan was the cause of his problem but said that he was nevertheless overcoming it. In addition to these facts, there were two reports from Urquhart to Fraser and a letter from Lawson to Urquhart in February of 1886 which are of particular interest.

In the first report Urquhart noted that Lawson was "going against" Swan in every way possible. He had met with Joseph Frank in Chicago and told him that Swan got thirty-five thousand dollars, in addition to the six thousand dollars he had paid Lawson, out of the original companies and that Lawson was asking for a statement of account.[20] He added the following charges so that nothing might be overlooked:

> He has also told Mr. Mckenzie [*sic*] some things he heard about the Ogalalla Cattle Co., in which Mr. M is heavily interested, also, about the South Omaha Land Syndicate & Stock Yards, and why Mr. Swan has dropped out of the Directorate of the two latter—In fact he has told him everything he knows that will damage the old man with his friends in Scotland.[21]

This report was followed three days later by another, informing Fraser that Swan had to pay Zack Thomason twenty thousand dollars more than he intended and that he had paid Lawson twelve thousand dollars more than intended for the stock of the Wyoming Hereford Association. Urquhart added, "I only give this information in order that you may be prepared for any proposition Swan may make," and he concluded that he did not think it was right to have "a man like that" managing the company.[22]

[20] *Ibid.*
[21] Urquhart to Fraser, February 8, 1886.
[22] Urquhart to Fraser, February 11, 1886.

The latter report was apparently the result of a letter from Lawson, dated February 8, 1886, which he forwarded to Fraser:

My Dear Bob

The old man has tumbled to the racket & I received my Hereford shares this moy [morning].

He has sent me 125 instead of 120. I wish to sell shares right off! What can I get for them? Can you sell them? Write and give me an idea what to do with them, & what they are likely to realize on the market.

A H S knuckles down in good form & talks of his "*honor.*" Did you know? [*sic*] he kept a heavy stock of that on hand. It is the first time ever I saw it on the surface. Write me soon with all particulars.

Yours faithfully
Thomas Lawson[23]

In light of these facts and the subsequent events, it is not difficult to understand why Swan felt that there was a concentrated effort to destroy him. Thomas Drimmie, by allowing the bank to bring suit against Swan for the note, did start the collapse of Alexander Swan. That Drimmie intended this to be the outcome is difficult to prove. At any rate, the first two events of that year—the case against the vendors and the failure of Swan Brothers—appear far from coincidental.

Swan's claim that he could still pay off one hundred cents on the dollar was judged by Dun as "sheer nonsense," and he added that it was "scarcely possible that any man could have ruined himself more senselessly, wildly and hopelessly" but that "with all his faults it was curious how

---

[23] Lawson to Urquhart, February 8, 1886.

down to the last so many people continued to have faith in him."[24] Dun suggested that all shares in the company registered to Swan be retained by the company and that Swan's salary cease as of the date of his suspension. It was discovered that Swan owed the company $3,497 and that he had signed a company note with Beveridge, Richards and Company for $10,807, which he used for his own purposes. Other such transactions appeared as the summer wore on. There was also the matter of fifty bulls that Thomas Lawson had sold Swan for the company but which Swan refused to accept. This only increased the animosity between the two men. Nevertheless, Lawson claimed a debt of $1,050 against the company, but after threatened lawsuits by both parties, this debt was eventually settled.

After about a week on the scene Dun discovered that Erasmus Nagle had been appointed receiver for Swan Brothers, which would upset the attachments by the First National Bank of Cheyenne and Joseph Frank. Alexander and Thomas Swan who "since 1872 have never had a balance sheet made out, or known how they stood had dissolved their partnership."[25] The financial condition of Swan Brothers had stood at $750,000 in liabilities and $155,000 in assets, but few people believed that Swan Brothers really had that much in assets. Swan himself was doing all he could to pay off the Beveridge note of $10,807. There was a note on the Wyoming Hereford Association for $20,-000 which the association would have to make good.[26] The

---

[24] The following narrative is based on a series of reports by Finlay Dun from Wyoming in the summer of 1887. "Reports, Finlay Dun in Wyoming June 8, October 2, 1887." Hereafter cited as "Dun Reports."

[25] *Ibid.*, June 19, 1887.

[26] Thomas Swan was president of the Wyoming Hereford Association; Alexander Swan was treasurer.

purchase of the "O7" by Rufe Rhodes from Swan for $500 had never been reported to the company, although Rhodes had a bank draft as proof of purchase. Early in June, Dun received notice from Swift and Campbell that the suit against Swan on guaranty and fraud combined was about to commence and that an attachment should be made on the firm, even though there was no hope of any monetary return.

Swan had been under "large and often complicated transactions" with Waixell, Van Tassell, Bosler, the Hillsdales, and nearly every other corporation or individual with which the company dealt.[27] Many of these owed the company money or would have to stand good for notes which they had undersigned for Swan as manager of the company. All were solvent and would have to pay their financial obligation to the company.

It would appear that Swan was, if nothing else, guilty of embezzlement, and Dun so informed the board: "He has been guilty of breach of trust and embezzlement and criminal charges might at any time be brought against him." However, there was really no point in so doing, for nothing could be gained in the matter; also embezzlement charges might well damage the company's case against the vendors.

It seemed incredible to the board in Scotland that embezzlement, manipulation with the calf brand, or any similar activity by Swan could have gone unnoticed by the bookkeeper, F. W. Lafrentz, or by the foremen. However, their loyalty to the company was attested to time and time again by Dun. Swan, they well knew, was careless and neglectful, but his credit and his "plausibility" were so

[27] "Dun Reports," July 25, 1887.

commanding that even after his return from Scotland in May he had managed to borrow twenty-six thousand dollars from Joseph Frank, ten thousand dollars from John Adams, and ten thousand dollars from Hicks of the First National Bank in Cheyenne—all without giving security.[28]

The company's financial difficulties could not be relieved by Swan, for he was now in receivership. Only those associated with him could, if the cases were proved, aid the company financially.

Perhaps of greatest importance was a thorough knowledge of just what the company's assets and liabilities were. Although Swan had been careless in the business of the company, he did develop it into a good, well-organized, and capable operation. The men on the ranch were regarded by Dun, and later by John Clay, as some of the best in the country. Animals, buildings, and equipment were all in good condition.

Board members still felt an insecurity, especially in regard to land titles. The Alien Land Act of March, 1887, had caused them again to seek full and definitive proof on their land titles. Corlett and Dun, shortly after Dun's arrival from Scotland, spent two full days going over the land book. Most of the titles were sound. The Union Pacific lands had been contracted for before passage of the 1887 Alien Land Act, and the company's title was "indisputable." There were some seventeen thousand acres of land to which the titles were doubtful or at least not clear. The land troubles affected the desert entries almost exclusively. Swan had had several of his friends from Iowa make entries in their names for the company. Many of them were reluctant to travel to Wyoming to establish the final proofs. Six people

[28] *Ibid.*, July 29, 1887.

from Indianola, Iowa, representing some twenty-two thousand acres of desert entries, did come to Wyoming at the company's expense (six hundred to seven hundred dollars) to prove up on their entries. Others who had taken out entries in their names for the company and upon whose lands the company had spent, in some instances, considerable money in improvement, were now reluctant to turn over the lands. Scarcely any of the claims involved legal problems. The problems were those of good faith.

Before the summer was over, however, Dun discovered that the difficulty of the land titles was more complex:

> It is easy to see the mistakes which have been in the land business—filings have been taken haphazzard [sic] from the map and made with very imperfect sometimes without any examination of the land; ditches have been cut where there was no water to put in them, and apparently occasionally platted without use of the level . . . repeatedly filings have been made and no further action until six or eight weeks of the date of proving up.[29]

He cautioned against altering the agreement between the company and the Union Pacific Railroad. That agreement was to defer all payments on the principal for five years and pay only the interest of 6 per cent a year.

Not only did the company have trouble getting parties to prove up on their claims and sign them over to the company but there were also trespassers. Dun and Al Bowie discovered several instances of both cattle and sheep trespassing on their range. One particularly large flock of about six thousand belonging to Peter Pompell was grazing on the railroad lands and had ruined them as winter feed for

[29] *Ibid.*, August 16, 1887.

the cattle. In some cases, small herdsmen were fencing in company land for their own use. Dun, Corlett, Bowie, and the other foremen obtained grazing leases from those they felt were not interfering with the company's grazing and instituted court proceedings against those who did not lease or move on voluntarily.

The greatest difficulty, both in the summer of 1887 and for years after, was in determining the number and kinds of cattle scattered over its ranges. The suit against the vendors depended upon some concrete proof of the numbers on the range. Swan had deemed it impossible to count the cattle in 1883, and the company was forced to agree. In 1887 it felt obliged to count the cattle, but it was just as impossible as it would have been four years earlier. There were two ways to attempt the count. The first was the calf brand, which had been the method relied on so far. The actual number of calves branded was, of course, tallied; however, the number of cows in the herd was estimated by setting a percentage of calves to cows. The calf brand did not classify the cattle except by estimation. After a period of years of actual counting and careful bookkeeping on the kinds of animals sold to the market, a cattleman could have a fair estimation of the size of his herd—provided, of course, that his percentages of birth and losses and his ratios of bulls to cows were approximately correct. The second method of counting the cattle was to count and mark each animal wearing a Swan brand, and even then there was no way of knowing if all had been counted.

Dun and the various foremen attempted both, and it was good that they did, for between the two methods a reasonably accurate accounting was made. The calf brands for 1885 and 1886 were known. A large discrepancy between the number of calves reported as branded in 1883–84 and the number branded in 1885–87 could constitute evidence of a fraudulent calf count. An attempt to gather information on the original numbers of the herd and the calf brands of 1883 and 1884 proved to be "mere surmise and common report."[30] No records were kept by the foremen. They turned all their accounts over to Swan or Lafrentz, and no one except Swan himself tallied up the various reports. He kept no figures; therefore, his reports to the company in those years were the only records available.

The calf brand of 1887 began with anticipated losses. The losses proved heavier as the roundups progressed. By the end of June the roundup in the Medicine Bow range was reporting heavy winter losses. Rhodes estimated that across the Swan ranches the losses were 25 per cent, and in one particular area of the Medicine Bow probably 50 per cent. The calf brand was off about one-third in all herds, including those of the company. Roundup 28, working west of the Platte and south of Fort Steele, reported 40 to 50 per cent fewer cattle and the calf brand as 25 to 50 per cent under average.[31] Time did not improve the early indications. Early in August a calf brand of twelve thousand was hopefully predicted; a week later the estimate was down to nine thousand. A 50 per cent drop in the calf brand in the Bates Hole area led Dun to conclude:

> Hundreds of weakly old cows, and their calves have perished and the tally demonstrates heavy mortality of two year old heifers pulled down by too early breeding. North and West of the Platte River throughout the northern parts of

[30] *Ibid.*, June 17, 1887.
[31] *Ibid.*, June 17, July 16, July 25, September 29, 1887.

the Territory and onwards through Montana losses as indicated were worse. Several outfits after traveling with the round-up and finding scarcely any cattle pulled out and went home; the northern winter losses are currently stated at 50% and exceptional cases are even higher.[32]

Late in September the calf brand was completed. For 1886 it had been 16,035 and for 1887 it was 8,800.

A comparison of these calf brands for 1886 and 1887 confirms the opinion, which I have repeatedly expressed, that the serious shortages of the present years, alike in calves and other cattle, had occurred throughout the plains in the mountains and foothills. Breeding stock suffer from winter and other hardships much more than dry stock, and hence the calf brand shrunk much more than the beef gather.[33]

The severe weather was also much harder on Texas cattle than on native stock. Of the 11,500 Texas steers the company had put on the range in 1884–85, Dun predicted that not more than 2,500 to 3,000 would be found.

Dun's major enterprise was counting all the Swan cattle. To do this he experimented with various types of paints with which to mark the animals. A mixture of lampblack, varnish for painting ironwork, and turpentine was eventually decided upon. The roundup crews marked all the Swan cattle they could find. At first Dun kept the tally but later entrusted part of the job to the foremen. That this new mixture for marking the cattle that had been counted was not "sufficiently adhesive" was made abundantly clear by the ditty

[32] *Ibid.*, August 11, 1887.

[33] *Ibid.* To this paragraph Fraser penned the following comment. "One would think Dun was making out a case for the Defenders in the shortage suit."

> Daddy Dun's a dandy
> But his paint won't stick.

Dun, throughout the summer, defended his method of tallying and was reluctant, even petulant, at the board's insistence on employing an independent person to count the cattle. He nevertheless gave way and turned the job over to James C. Johnston. Johnston's report on the tally established the hopelessness of counting all the cattle.[34] He had told Dun when he took over on July 24 that marking the cattle on the left hip with a streak of blue paint would not work. The heat, rain, and bumping of cattle against one another wore the mark off before the summer was over. It was impossible to tally a herd of such size, which had scattered over such a vast area in one year. The only possible way of counting the cattle was to rebrand all of them; even then some would be missed. However, such a method would do more damage by loss of weight from disturbing the cattle than could be gained from the tally. Johnston recommended that an estimate be made according to a rule of thumb—a custom on the range of multiplying the number of calves by five. Depending on whether the year represented a good or bad calf brand, 10 to 20 per cent off the whole number could be deducted.

The actual number of cattle counted by Dun's method was 29,008. Johnston first used that figure and arbitrarily estimated that 22.5 per cent had not been counted; therefore, the total number of cattle on the range should have been 37,400, not including calves or fall shipments. By applying the calf-brand test the number should have been

---

[34] "Report on cattle by James C. Johnston, October 15, 1887." Johnston later became chairman of the board of Swan Land and Cattle Company, Ltd., and after that manager of the Prairie Cattle Company.

36,196, again not including calves or fall shipments. Like Dun, Johnston agreed that any sort of estimate, and probably even a rebranding of the herd, would be of no benefit to the case against the vendors.[35]

The Swan Land and Cattle Company Limited vs. *Joseph Frank, et al.*, went to trial July 22, 1889, in the United States Court for the Northern District of Illinois, and in it appeared no test of Johnston's or Dun's prediction on the use of the tally as evidence.[36] Swift and Campbell prepared a long bill of complaint, in which suit was taken against Joseph Frank and about fifteen other trustees and shareholders, including Alexander H. Swan, of the original companies. The complaint was made on the grounds that, since the corporations no longer existed and there was no officer of the companies against whom action could be taken, the shareholders were the proper parties. All the parties to the suit, with the exception of Swan, who was residing in Wyoming, were within the jurisdiction of the court. Having established the jurisdiction of the court and the validity of responsibility on the part of the original companies for the guarantee of the number of cattle, the company, by using the calf brand of the several consecutive years 1883 to 1887, attempted to prove that the number of cattle guaranteed did not actually exist at the time of the sale. The plaintiff asked for compensation of eight hundred thousand dollars for a deficiency of some thirty-two thousand head of cattle.

The basis of the company's evidence in the suit—the calf brand—was not challenged by the defendants and only briefly alluded to by the court. The defendants, represented by the firm of Kraus, Mayer and Stein, of Chicago,

---

[35] *Ibid.*

[36] *Swan Land & Cattle Co., Ltd.* vs. *Joseph Frank, et al.*, 148 U.S. 603.

and J. W. Woolworth, of Omaha, presented a brief demurrer, in which they challenged the right of the company to bring suit against the parties as shareholders and trustees.[37] Judge Blodgett agreed with the defendants: "It would be anomalous and unjust, it seems to me, to try this question in a suit to which the corporations were not parties, and where they could not be heard."[38]

The bill was against the wrong party, the judge continued, and the case should have been brought against the companies. Moreover, the court should have determined the amount of compensation due, if any. However: "These vendor corporations, being Wyoming Corporations, cannot be brought into this court, and hence the bill is not only fatally defective, as it stands, but cannot be amended in that respect."[39]

Although Swift and Campbell gave every assurance that they could win the case, they did not. The very elements which made their case defective, as outlined by the judge, would have prevented any other bill from being drawn. In short, Swift and Campbell tried the only case in which compensation could be obtained. A case against the original companies tried in Wyoming and based upon "book count" and "calf brands," following the bad winter of 1886–87, would have been useless. Also, very few, if any, of the trustees or shareholders of the original companies in Wyoming had any capital from which monetary compensation could have been gained.

As the devastating effects of the winter began to materi-

---

[37] *Ibid.*
[38] *Swan Land and Cattle Co., Ltd.* vs. *Frank et al.*, July 22, 1889. *Federal Reporter*, Vol. XXXIX, No. 9, (September 24, 1889), 461.
[39] *Ibid.*, 461–62.

alize, the cattle industry realized that great changes were necessary. Both Dun and the company, as well as hundreds of other cattlemen, began thoughtful consideration and alteration of their ranching scheme. Some, of course, were wiped out by the winter storms and never tried to regain their losses. Throughout the summer Dun evaluated and considered the future policy and management of the company. There was no serious consideration of liquidating the company; the future depended on how to best conserve company assets and re-establish its financial position. This meant cutting down operating cost, preserving and protecting its greatly depleted herds, and discovering some means of making it all more profitable.

Immediately the interim manager began reducing operating cost. The surveyor, John A. Apperson, who had been employed by Swan on an annual basis, was dismissed and placed on a small retainer. Many of the errors in land titles were later found to be his fault. The company made every effort not to antagonize the surveyor, since his favorable testimony would be necessary in proving many land titles. Billy Swan, Alexander Swan's son, was released as the shipping clerk. The salary was not much, but Dun thought it only a sinecure. On the Little Medicine Bow so many visitors, travelers, and loafers stopped over in the summer that Bowie and Dun agreed it was necessary to charge for meals, bedding, and care of animals.

During the summer Dun had, from time to time, speculated on the future management of the company. In line with reducing the cost of operation and in light of the reduced number of cattle, he recommended that Lafrentz and Al Bowie, along with about thirty cowhands, could handle the company's affairs. Of Al Bowie, Dun said, "He is an infinitely better cowman than Swan ever was."[40] Dun could spend the summers in Wyoming and winters in Edinburgh. George Prentice, Jr., could take Dun's place in Wyoming during the winters. Thus the company could save at least the ten-thousand-dollar annual salary to the manager. That arrangement would have been economical and probably to Dun's satisfaction, but the company needed a more permanent arrangement.

The year 1887 was a year of desperation for the Swan Company. The company realized that the anticipated profit was not being returned, and it began first to seek the reasons and then the solution. The reasons were various, but the foremost one appeared to be a shortage of cattle. There is no more evidence available now than there was then to determine the true cause of the cattle shortage. It can be concluded however, that the original number of cattle sold to the Swan Company was short. The number short cannot be determined, nor can it be proved that Alexander Swan intentionally overstated the number. Fraud could not be proved in 1887; it cannot be proved now.

Alexander Swan went bankrupt. It may have been as a result of his own mismanagement or it may have been as a result of some behind-the-scene manipulation by members of the board and other parties. It appears that Swan was careless with certain financial matters, both company and private. That was his style. It also appears that the board, if it did not perpetrate the error, certainly capitalized on it. The illuminating fact is that Swan's personal friends, whether on the board in Scotland or the many boards of the other Swan progenies, could have come to

[40] "Dun Reports," June 8, June 17, July 23, 1887.

his aid. They did not. Swan could have been saved, but he was not.

The best possible reason for this sad conclusion is that Swan was the one person, in so many of the organizations he had helped create, who could be sacrificed. His investments were too small and too scattered to ruin any of them. He also obviously had enemies—some because of envy, others because of a sense of persecution.

The shareholders were hurt not only by the failure of the anticipated profit but also by the great loss of cattle in the winter of 1886–87 and the constant call for more money. Consequently, they sought some relief. Swan was that relief, even the scapegoat, and they were willing to blame him for their problems. This may have eased their consciences, but it did little for the squeeze on their purses. No money was to be had from Swan.

The company turned next to a critical examination of its own resources and discovered it was the possessor of a great investment that could neither yield immediate returns nor be liquidated immediately. The promise was still there, but for the present the company had to find a way to hold on to what it had.

CHAPTER V

Reorganization
at Home and Abroad

THE FALL of 1887 found the shareholders anxiously examining the results of the past year. The company's assets in land, cattle, and shares had declined. The company had suffered but survived, and soon its directors would seek out a cause and, they hoped, a culprit. But for the moment the company was more concerned with its future than its past. That future involved two things: the range and the company—the future value of the company's assets in cattle and land and the fiscal structure and organization of the company. Although the two were different aspects of the same business, they were totally dependent upon each other. It was a simple matter of assets and liabilities.

The company had several alternatives it could follow. It could sink more money into the operation; but to throw good money after bad was both poor policy and unpopular economics. It could write off a portion of its capital as lost, a procedure allowed by the Articles of Association. It could liquidate if one-half of the capital was lost. The last possibility was quickly discarded, and the company was left with the decision which of the remaining alternatives it would follow.

Dun's reports from the ranch in 1887 provided at least a basis for what the future of the range should be. The heavy death toll during the winter of 1886–87 was attributed primarily to inadequate winter provisions for the cattle and to the overstocking of the range. It was now clear that better winter provisions must be made for the cattle. Only the small herds for which food and shelter had been provided survived the winter without loss. Rufe Rhodes, the Swan Company foreman, believed that no herd could be kept in Wyoming without provision for winter feed: "Without such food one is liable some years to lose one half the stock. The men who have 500 cattle and look after them . . . in the long run are better off than those who have 1,500 and nothing for them in winter."[1] In Dun's opinion, suitable winter quarters would not only reduce the death toll on range cattle but also provide other benefits:

Conditions gained during summer would thus be conserved through winter: from our breeding females 75% of calves would be branded; our three year old steers would realize $10.00 per head more than they can do under present circumstances, and make beef worthy the name. Successful cattlemen in Wyoming must gradually come to such management.[2]

Rhodes and other cattlemen were of the opinion that the range was accommodating all the cattle it could. Barbed wire, sheep, and settlers had so restricted the use of the range that it had become overstocked. Overstocking con-

[1] "Dun Reports," July 4, 1887. (Unless otherwise indicated, all citations in this chapter are from the Swan Files of the WRCIS.
[2] *Ibid.*, October 2, 1887.

tributed to the losses of 1886–87. However, the problem of overstocking had been taken care of by natural conditions during the previous winter.

Overstocking was not the only cause for losses. Dun discovered others. Heavy losses had occurred in the higher-grade cattle, and Dun believed that by spaying about a thousand high-grade heifers a more hardy breed could be produced. On the other hand, the older, lower-graded cattle were dying out from old age or were turning barren. These two factors, plus the better care the company had provided for the bulls, creating a surplus in that class, had caused a serious imbalance in the herds. The bulls were overbreeding the older stock and breaking down the heifers, causing considerable loss of cows and a reduced calf brand.[3] Dun offered no solution to the latter problem. Two of the immediate problems of the range appeared to be a readjustment of the different classes of cattle and better management of the herds.

James Tait again offered his recommendation to divide the range into a series of small, independently operated ranches, all working for the company. Dun agreed with the intent, but, like Swan and Bowie, he doubted its practicality on a range as large as that held by the company. In response to Tait's proposal to distribute the herds "under the charge of separate foremen on different ranches," Dun noted that this practice had already been adopted to some degree, especially in the winter. But the cowboy had a peculiar kind of loyalty and independence. The cowboy's loyalty to his ranch or to his foreman exceeded that to the company. Often it created competition instead of co-operation. A team or a horse borrowed from one ranch by another

[3] *Ibid.*, June 17, 1887.

was often literally worked to death, the loss falling to the ranch making the loan. The problem now was to get the men and foremen to regard all the property as that of the company and not that of their own independent ranches.

Dun thought that subdivision of the herds in the summer would be "inexpedient." Full value of the range could not be obtained under open range, where the herds could drift and feed at will, but any attempt to restrict the herds to artificial bounds would be impractical. A division of the range into different ranches for the summer simply would not be feasible.[4] While Dun faithfully recorded his observations on the range and commented on the opinions of others, he failed to offer any range policy beyond the reduction in the grade of cattle and establishment of better winter conditions.

James C. Johnston, in his report on the cattle count, also made recommendations for the future. He, like Dun, did not agree with artificial boundaries, but he did suggest a division of the range along a more natural line. The range east of the mountains should be used for steers and spayed heifers, because the better climate and feed would serve to finish the herds for market. The range west of the mountains should be used for the breeding stock during the spring and summer. These suggestions, to a large extent, were followed by Clay when he became manager. This division of the herds would also allow the working of the market-bound cattle without harm to the calves and heavy cows, while the working of the cow herd would not reduce the weight of the feed stock.[5]

In brief, Dun, Tait, and Johnston, as well as the foremen

[4] *Ibid.*, October 2, 1887.
[5] James C. Johnston, "Report on Cattle," October 15, 1887.

on the range and other cattlemen in the area, agreed that something would have to be done about the wintering of cattle and the closing of the range and that more attention must be given to the business of cattle raising. Governor Thomas Moonlight echoed these convictions:

> My opinion of all the ranches is, that the day of success is passed away unless a man's interest remains permanently on each ranch and devotes his whole time, and gives his whole attention to the business. Everything is going to decay naturally, houses, fences, buildings and implements and even the grasses.[6]

Compounding the problems of reorganizing the herds and providing winter feed was the low price of beef. Cattle prices had been in a depressed condition since 1883. The virtual destruction of the beef-producing herds on the northern plains would seem to limit the supply of beef for the market and force prices up. This, unfortunately, did not happen. All the ranges had been overstocked, and drought in the southern plains caused a heavy marketing of beef from that area. Philip Armour, testifying before a Senate committee in 1889, listed the leading cause of the decline in cattle values:

> ... over-production and over-marketing of cattle, especially of that grade of cattle known as range or Southwestern cattle. The over-marketing of cattle has been brought about by the reckless investment and speculation in ranch properties, which placed a fictitious value upon cattle and resulted eventually in withdrawal of money so invested, thus com-

[6] "Report of Governor Moonlight to Department of Interior for the year 1888," reprinted in *Wyoming: The 75th Year*, Douglas, June, 1965, 202.

pelling many engaged in the business, to permanently market their cattle, to realize on them.[7]

Other causes for the decline were low prices of hides, the oleomargarine controversy, quarantine laws, and huge cattle-raising enterprises in South America, Australia, and New Zealand.[8]

Overmarketing, reckless investment, poor management, and overstocking of the range all contributed to the unfortunate circumstances of the cattle industry, but the real core of the problem was the manner in which the cattle industry had suddenly boomed in 1882–83. The *Laramie Daily Boomerang* of July 29, 1886, reported on the extent of foreign investments. According to the American consul at Dundee, Scotland, eleven Scottish and English companies owned over two million acres in the United States. Another million and a half were leased by them at less than five cents an acre. These eleven companies owned some seven hundred thousand head of cattle and had sold nearly ninety thousand in 1885. Yet, for all this, none of the foreign companies had paid more than a 10 per cent dividend, and nearly half of them had paid no dividend at all.

It appeared that the foreign investor must assume responsibility for the unsound condition of the cattle industry in proportion to the amount of his investment. But in some cases, either out of ignorance or apathy, he exercised such loose control over the operation of the range that he must be regarded as victim rather than villain.

The British cattlemen's views on the future of the range

[7] Philip Armour, "The Present Condition of the Live Cattle and Beef Markets of the United States, and the Causes Therefore," *Statement of Philip D. Armour before the Special Committee of the United States Senate.* Chicago, Chicago Legal News Co., 1889.

[8] *Ibid.*

were expressed in an article in the *Boston Daily Advertiser*. Those views reached Thomas Sturgis by way of the *Boston Journal*. In behalf of the leading cattlemen of Cheyenne, Sturgis responded in the *Laramie Daily Boomerang*:

> The repeated mention of the word Englishmen and their opinions provokes a smile among cattlemen here for the following reasons: In the first place, it conveys the idea they constitute the greater part of the cattle raising community and second, that their opinions are of value.[9]

He spent the next few columns discounting both such assumptions. In the first place, there were approximately 450 members in the Wyoming Stock Growers' Association, and of that number only fourteen were interested in or connected with foreign companies. "The interest of foreign capital in the vast section of country our association covers is therefore three per cent." In the second place, the average American enterprise had been far more successful than the foreign. "Their business in many instances has been to them a grand picnic." The foreign cattlemen knew little about the business, they stayed in America only a short period of time each year, and "their views, taken as a body, would not be conceded, for a moment to have the weight that would be attached to those of the practical American."[10]

Any idea that the cattle business was doomed had little place in the actual circumstances. In Sturgis' opinion, the "Laramie Englishmen's sphere of vision is limited to a very

---

[9] *Daily Boomerang* (Laramie), December 30, 1886. This is a long letter and one of the more interesting items on the foreign investor and his position among the local cattlemen. It also appears to overemphasize the importance of the American cattlemen, and the figures appear to apply more to the number of cattlemen than to amount of land and cattle.

[10] *Ibid.*

small section of country and bears an infinitesimally small proportion, and has even less applicability, to the vast ranges of territory."[11] The heavy losses that had occurred were primarily in the Texas cattle brought in during the fall. The cattle market had been low, but the low prices applied to all beef and not just to that of the high-plains cattle. None of the local cattlemen believed that the numerous liquidations that followed were going to take place. The British, Sturgis felt, simply had been too greedy. They had bought in when things looked most promising and expected returns of 15 and 20 per cent, which were not realistic as long as the industry was still in a growing stage. In a sense, the British, who judged the business on the profit motive, had little idea of the real value of the industry or its future. Sturgis thought that the "Englishman's views, or rather his disappointments, are not shared in by the great bulk of cattle raisers of this country."[12] Sturgis obviously did not grant the British a representation on the range according to their investment, but rather according to their number. There were fewer British cattlemen than American; therefore, they had less right to say anything and less reason to be heard.

In 1897 the United States Bureau of Animal Husbandry summed up the conditions of the cattle business over the preceding several years for the benefit of the Congress of the United States:

> About seven years ago the price of cattle—then all grades, and comparatively at a high figure—began to decline. The reasons were obvious. Up to that time most, if not all, of the herds roaming over the vast plains and uplands of the range

[11] *Ibid.*
[12] *Ibid.*

states in the Far West had been kept as "breeding stock," and the result was that they accumulated in such numbers that there was an overproduction—the supply became greater than the demand.[13]

The stock owners then went back to maintaining "steer herds," spaying heifers, and shipping calves until 1893, when they determined there might be a cow famine. From that time on they commenced to build producing herds. Overproduction was not likely to occur again, since homesteading and pre-emption had broken up the unlimited government graze, and owners now had to account and provide for all their cattle.[14]

Regardless of who or what was responsible for the unrewarding state of the cattle industry, it was the financier, both American and foreign, who had to bear the misfortunes. While the concern of the company for affairs on the range, for the shelter and feeding of the cattle, for the cattle market, for the improvement of herds or consolidation of their holdings was of immediate and significant importance, the affairs of the company in Edinburgh were even more distressing.

At an extraordinary general meeting on March 12, 1886, the shareholders had passed a resolution to raise the company's capital to £900,000 by creating fifteen thousand £10 preference shares upon the assumption that the capital would be used to pay for the lands purchased from the Union Pacific Railroad. The money was not used for that purpose, however, and considerable discontent resulted.

---

[13] U.S. Congress, House, *The Cattle Industry of Colorado, Wyoming and Nevada and the Sheep Industry of Colorado in 1897*, by John T. McNeely, 55th Cong., 3rd sess., *House Doc., No. 307*, 377–81.

[14] *Ibid.*

Alexander Hamilton Swan

The Chug Store and Hotel, a stage stop for the Cheyenne and
Black Hills stage

The manager's residence, office, and store at Chugwater

The headquarters at Chugwater

The Hi Kelly Ranch at Chugwater

Ranch on the Chugwater, two views

The M Bar Ranch house

The Bard Ranch house

Box Elder Canyon showing perspective of Goshen Hole

A branch of Sybille Creek

A traction engine breaking sod in Chugwater Valley

Shearing Pens Ranch at shearing season. One million pounds of wool are stacked between the barn and the house.

Shearing Pens Ranch. The sheep in the foreground are ready for shearing.

The bed grounds behind the shearing pens

Roping a steer to inspect the brand

Branding a maverick

Roundup crew at noon meal

THE SWAN LAND AND CATTLE CO. (Limited.)

A. H. SWAN, General Manager.

ALEXANDER BOWIE, General Foreman.

P. O. address, Cheyenne, Wyo.

Ranges, North Platte, Sheep Creek, Laramie River, Medicine Bow, Sabile and Chugwater, Wyoming and Nebraska.

Also own the following brands:

OR Wattle on left shoulder. **7** Wattle on left neck. **ꓶ** Wattle on right neck.

Ⴍ Wattle on right neck. **∩** Wattle on ham of cows. **E** Road brand.

TY Also **O** on left hip. **O** Wattle on left neck.

F on left side and hip; crop and split both ears. **L L** Overslope right and split left ear.

60 Split left ear. **VO** Underbit right, overbit left ear. ** XX** Split both ears.

⩒   ⱶO   7⌐l   H⌶H   TOM   J

IOU   ⌐   CAR   J   Ê   ⋃P   ↑

J3   CC   ⌒   ⦂⦂ᵢ left shoulder and **=** hip.

S   HCO   G   ZIL   D   ⊔

7K on left side and **∩** on hip. **L—   =   FS**

7l   NN   SN   ∩   07   N—   ¢

H   LO   ⌐N   A   20   5 left side and hip.

ICC Crop and split right and swallowfork left ear. **L/R** on left side and **=** left hip.

∩ on left side and **ઠ** left hip. **O   ICC** Crop and split right, swallowfork left ear.

I—   26 on left side and **=** hip. **49   M   HD**

7T on left side and **=** left hip. **Q** **IX** left side and hip.

ASH   ⍭ on left side and **=** left hip. **I3   ⌒**

The Swan Land and Cattle Company brands

THE SWAN LAND AND CATTLE CO.—Continued.

66 on left side and ⌐ left hip.   ⋈ on left side and ⌐ left hip.

76 on left side and ⌐ left hip.   75 on left side and ⌐ left hip.   O<

V   M on left side and R left hip.   I=   F left shoulder and thigh.

M̄   MK on left side and ⋀ left hip.   I M NA 40

⫣ ⋔ ⊥ ∴ ⋎ 78 on left side and ⌐ left hip.

All calves branded after January, 1884, same as cut.

Horse brands, same as cut, and ⎍ 07 ⋏ ⫣

Graded stock.

Also own 96

Horse brand, H left shoulder.

SWAN, CHESIRE & CO.

T. J. SWAN, Manager.

P. O. address, Cheyenne, Wyo.
Range, Hat Creek, Laramie County, Wyo.
Brand, same as cut on both sides.
Also own ,22   2̄2̄

RH ⊃⤙⊂ BOX POX ℍ

Horse brands, 22 and ⊃⤙⊂

From the *Wyoming Stock Growers' Association Brand Book,* 1884

"Rounding 'Em Up!"

At the annual meeting in March, 1887, it was the major topic of discussion, and the directors were heavily criticized. The shareholders had not received a dividend the previous year and were anxious about the future.

One large shareholder, Thomas Landale, led the attack upon the directors. He accused them of using the idea of paying for the railroad lands only as a means of increasing the capital and then using the money for whatever purpose they desired. The urgency of paying for the railroad lands had resulted from the proposed alien bill, which would prevent foreigners and foreign companies from holding lands in America (the bill in the meantime had been passed —see Chapter VI). The directors, however, had used the money to buy the controversial Reel herd and ranch. Landale proposed that a committee of shareholders be appointed to meet with the directors and that the report not be adopted until they had heard from their American counsel on the suit against the vendors. The directors, in their defense, explained that too few of the preference shares had been taken up to pay for the railroad lands, and they considered that the other items were more important than the lands purchased from the Union Pacific, since a concession had been obtained from the railroad company for deferment of payment.[15]

Nothing occurred during 1887 to improve the attitude of the shareholders. Early in December they received a report from the directors on the activities of the company to date. The report was the result of Finlay Dun's work of the summer, and the news was grim.[16] There would be no

---

[15] *Report of the Fourth Annual General Meeting*, March 17, 1887.
[16] See Chapter III above for discussion of the "Dun Reports."

dividend this year; heavy losses had been sustained, and calls would have to be made for more capital.

According to the figures of the directors, based on estimates and on Dun's partial tally of the cattle, the herd amounted to only 55,162 head. Even that estimate proved too high. It was based on a calf brand of 8,674. The breeding females were estimated at 45 per cent, or 19,276. But Dun had tallied only 10,765. Therefore, by taking the average of the number tallied and the number estimated for the breeding stock, the directors arrived at the total figure 55,162 for the herd. The cattle were valued at twenty-five dollars a head. The railroad lands were valued at one dollar an acre, patented lands at thirty dollars an acre, and all the land in the process of acquisition at ten dollars an acre. On this evaluation the company listed its principal assets at £505,338 and its principal liabilities at £277,390.[17]

The shareholders were summoned to meet on December 20, 1887, to hear an official reading of Dun's report. Since they had already seen copies of it, they were primarily concerned with what could be done about the situation. The company obviously had extensive and favorable property that was too valuable to liquidate at the present. Landale again led the assault upon the directors. He felt that a committee of shareholders ought to be appointed to meet with the directors before the report was adopted. A parliamentary compromise was arrived at whereby the report was "received" and a committee appointed, with Landale at its head.

The shareholders' committee met with the directors, examined the various reports and activities of the company and the managers, and early in 1888 issued a report to the

[17] "Director's Report to the Shareholders," December 7, 1887.

shareholders. The management of the company, both at home and in Wyoming, came under heavy fire:

> From what had previously transpired, and from the infor-
> mation we have since been able to acquire, we regret to say
> that, while the management at Wyoming appear to have
> been of the most careless and reckless character, the failure
> of the several Deputation, appointed for the very purpose
> of examining into the management of the Company's affairs
> at the Ranges, to detect the deceptions being practiced by
> the Manager, is most unfortunate.[18]

The first responsibility of the company's managers had been to fix the number of cattle to be paid for according to the calf brand of 1883, but, even with two deputations to the ranges that summer, "no steps were taken . . . until 1887 to verify the statements made by the Manager as to the number of calves branded by the Foremen." The directors had, after repeated warnings of shortages by Tait and others, and after repeated warnings of Swan's mismanagement, continued to report everything as satisfactory. The committee also discovered a shortage of four thousand acres of land for an additional loss of £20,000.[19]

The committee found the financial position of the company even more unsatisfactory. The 1886 issue of £100,000 worth of preference shares had been designed to provide £60,000 for railroad lands, £13,000 for the bank debt, and the remainder for working capital. Up to May, 1886, only £58,000 of the stock had been taken up, and the board had invested £13,917 in the Reel herd, £2,645 in railroad lands,

---

[18] "Report to the Shareholders of the Swan Land and Cattle Company, Limited, by the Committee Appointed at a General Meeting of Shareholders held 20th December 1887," not dated, but presented before the annual meeting of the company in March, 1887.

[19] *Ibid.*

and £20,677 on the bank overdraft. The balance had been spent for land and cattle, part of which had already been lost. The committee was severely critical of the manner in which the £58,000 had been used. As for the future policy of the company on the range, the members believed that more attention must be paid to winter shelter and feed for the cattle they already had, instead of more purchases of land and cattle. They concluded:

> In view of the past mismanagement, which had resulted in such deplorable and avoidable loss, we have, with much regret, and after much consideration, to state that we have no confidence in the present Board, and recommend to Shareholders to take what steps they think proper for its reconstruction.[20]

Before any reconstruction of the board took place, the shareholders were offered additional testimony on the incompetence of the present members, this time from Thomas Lawson.[21] The suit against the vendors had made Lawson appear a coconspirator of A. H. Swan, though he was not named in the suit. Such a position had given him no recourse at law, and so he had presented his plea to the directors, but they had neglected to inform the shareholders of the fact. Lawson stated his case in a sixteen-page printed letter to the shareholders. As for the management, Lawson believed:

> Whether, in short, the whole course of your Board of Managers, or a majority thereof, has not been such as to suggest, if not proven too much leniency, neglect, or worse, on their part, with the American Management, in a series of

[20] *Ibid.*
[21] Lawson's relationship with the Swan Company is covered in detail in Chapter III above.

transactions in which your Company has been victimized to the advantage of other concerns in which some of your directors possibly may have had outside interests.[22]

George Prentice, Colin J. Mackenzie, and especially Finlay Dun were singled out by Lawson for criticism.

Lawson reviewed the cattle industry in the States for the shareholders, noting that the industry was in a depressed state for a number of reasons, of which the "immediate and most disastrous were climatological." The winter of 1886–87 had "literally blotted out whole herds on the over-stocked ranges in Dakota, Montana, and Wyoming."[23] Climate was a natural cause and not one for which preparation could always be made, but mismanagement was different; someone must always be to blame. He further informed the shareholders: "It may be very nice and pleasant for you to get up a suit and have Mr. A. H. Swan and me made the butt of for the recrimination of angry shareholders, and under this cloud cover up your FIVE YEARS OF RUIN-OUS MISMANAGEMENT of the Company's property."[24]

To Lawson the board's mismanagement was not "very nice," and he offered several examples. Acceptance of the first year's calf brand from the man who guaranteed it was not good business practice. The book count of the company was probably short when it received the property. That was usual, but the company had bought the cattle from Swan for twenty-five dollars a head and could have sold them the same season for thirty dollars. Since that time they had

[22] Letter "To the Shareholders of the Swan Land and Cattle Company, Limited (Confidential and Private)," Granite Building, St. Louis, Mo., December 10, 1887, from Thomas Lawson. A postscript is added, dated December 31, 1887, to comment on the December 7 report of the company.
[23] *Ibid.*
[24] *Ibid.*

bought several herds by book count for more than they were worth because of a decline in the general market. Lawson did not believe that the company was hurt in the original purchases, but rather by poor management in the past five years. In addition, Lawson accused Mackenzie of paying Swan a commission on three or four Angus bulls purchased from Mackenzie to be used on the ranges.

Lawson reserved his most bitter criticism for Finlay Dun:

> You will of course have a "full, true and particular account" of Mr. Finlay Dun's ludicrous and abortive attempt to "talley-paint" the Company's cattle. . . . The attempt to account for the shrinkage of the herds from 120,000 to 50,000 head will be the occasion for some mathematical gymnastics which I shall be curious to witness. . . . I am afraid that Mr. Dun will find the writing of a report which shall be satisfactory to the shareholders and at the same time true, a more difficult undertaking than painting cattle in a first class cow punching burlesque.[25]

In a postscript Lawson added:

> When the practical cattle-man reflects for a moment that a person representing so vast an interest and occupying so responsible a position as that of Mr. Finlay Dun, toward the Swan Land and Cattle Company should undertake to count its enormous herds by a method so utterly inadequate as that adopted by Mr. Dun, the absurdity of the situation is uppermost; and when he reads Mr. Dun's plaintive statement "that the paint used did not prove sufficiently adhesive" he can scarcely forebear repeating the comment of the cowboys when they hear of the fiasco—"Old man Dun's a dandy, but his paint won't stick."[26]

[25] *Ibid.*   [26] *Ibid.*

Perhaps the most interesting point in Lawson's letter was his application of the formula used by the board in arriving at its current number of cattle by way of the calf brand for the preceding five years:[27]

Year	Calf brand	Book count of total number of herd	Dun's estimate of calf brand	Excess over book count	Shortage under book count
1883	19,344	108,763	122,953	14,190	
1884	21,428	121,211	136,270	15,059	
1885	20,104	123,460	127,862	4,402	
1886	14,824	124,127	82,617		41,510
1887	8,674		55,162		

If the method of calculating the herd on the basis of the calf brand was valid in 1887, it should have been true for any other year. If that was the case, then the number of cattle bought by the company was in excess of the number paid for by 14,190, instead of a shortage of some 20,000. Lawson concluded: "In the face of these damming [*sic*] figures, how can the Board explain their assertion in their present report that 'the diminution has been caused largely by the short delivery at the outset, and partly by losses which were not reported when they occurred'?"[28] While Lawson made no defense of Swan—he personally thought him totally incapable of managing the company—he believed that the board was even more responsible for the condition of the company, and perhaps even less capable

27 *Ibid.*
28 *Ibid.*

than Swan. In his view there was no defense for what had already been done, and it was impossible to defend the shortage suit on the same basis now used to evaluate the property of the company.

Although the company had instituted its suit against the vendors for shortages in the herd at the time of purchase and blamed their former manager for the predicament they were in, they were clearly as responsible as Swan. He was convincing and personable, but, like the board, his greatest offenses were neglect and overindulgence. They were all guilty of negligence, Swan in managing the ranges, the company directors in checking on the manager and managing the company. All overindulged in land and cattle, became too deeply involved in other affairs, and gambled for greater profit than circumstances warranted.

Since the members of the board were among the largest shareholders, whatever happened to them would be in greater proportion than to the smaller shareholders; consequently, it is difficult to believe that they had committed intentional errors. Nevertheless, at the next annual meeting Thomas Landale, Alexander McNab, Jr., and Thomas Swan, all members of the shareholders' committee, were nominated and elected to the board.[29]

In their annual report in 1889 the directors offered some proof about the value of their herds in the years discussed by Lawson. The cattle were carried on the books at $25 a head. For all animals sold—from fat steers to old bulls—the average price in 1884 was $40.67; in 1885, $33.80; in 1886, $26.34; in 1887, $26.22; and in 1888, $29.83. The portion of each class of animal sold in each year and the

[29] "Report of Fifth Annual General Meeting," April 7, 1888.

amounts received for them account for the differences in price. But the figures nonetheless offer some support to Lawson's charges about the value of cattle and about buying them high and selling low.[30]

In the summer of 1887, Alexander Swan had been dismissed as manager, and that position had been temporarily filled by Finlay Dun. Once the company had determined the major problems, it became imperative to find a permanent replacement for Swan. A person who was both well qualified in the financial management of the company and loyal to the home board would not be easy to find. As mentioned earlier, Robert Urquhart was working in the Cheyenne office at the time Swan was dismissed. In a letter to the secretary he requested the manager's position, even offering to take a lower salary. In another letter the same day, this time to his friend William Fraser, he requested an appointment as cashier to replace F. W. Lafrentz.[31]

His requests were ignored, and shortly after the first of the year the board began its search for a manager. Finlay Dun and James C. Johnston were candidates. The board requested the advice of the American attorneys Swift and Campbell. In a letter from William Swift to William Fraser, marked "confidential," Swift outlined the future of the cattle business.

As Swift saw it, the cattle business in 1888 needed the same skill and ability as any other established business. The cattle industry was and would continue to be beset by special difficulties. Companies would have trouble obtaining patents on land already entered; alien owners would

---

[30] "Report by Directors to the Sixth Annual General Meeting," March 26, 1889.

[31] Urquhart to Fraser, May 16, 1887, and Dun to Fraser, May 16, 1887, in "Dun Reports." See Chapter III above for discussion of Urquhart.

always be at a disadvantage; the days of free public grazing were drawing to a close, and new methods of operation would have to be developed. Moreover, the idea of "cattle barons" was displeasing to the American press. Despite these problems, however, Swift believed the outlook for the cattle business was better than it had been for several years. The losses of the winter of 1886–87, though severe, ultimately would benefit those who survived. They would be "actually benefited by the losses of others, as the competition will be much less for several years."[32]

A few days later Swift made his recommendations to the committee of shareholders. Finlay Dun would not be acceptable as a manager, Swift said. He did not seem to have the necessary ability and he had made mistakes in his interim appointment—especially the mistake of being too friendly with Swan's cronies. The other candidate, James C. Johnston, Swift and Campbell did not know well enough to make a recommendation. Instead, they recommended John Clay, Jr., of Chicago, and concluded:

> We will, however, add generally, that the property of your company holds a leading position in Wyoming, and the man who is its Manager, will be looked up to by the other cattle men, and he should be able, either alone, or in combination with others to look after the cattle interests as affected by legislation in the Territory and at Washington, as well as superintend the more immediate business of the ranch. The property of the Company is a good one. . . . But the failure or success of the Company rests almost solely with the man whom you make Manager.[33]

---

[32] Swift to Fraser, February 22, 1888.
[33] Swift and Campbell to Thomas Landale, Chairman of the Committee of Shareholders, Chicago, March 1, 1888.

Although Clay was not an applicant, the board offered him the position. "The reason I was eventually selected was not that I was a better man than my friend Johnston, but that I was able to give valuable financial assistance to the Company."[34] Clay's efforts were not altogether successful. In his words, "For eight years I seemed to be climbing, fighting, quarreling, making gigantic efforts to produce prosperity out of poverty and accomplishing very little."[35]

The company gradually improved its financial position under Clay's direction, however. His policy was to economize. When he took over as manager, he found a full, highly efficient crew, capable of running one hundred thousand cattle. For this he rather reluctantly gave credit to Alexander Swan. There was a general headquarters, a cattle headquarters, and a farming headquarters. There were nine cooks and helpers on the various ranches—all of whom Clay dismissed except the cook at the ranch headquarters. Al Bowie, the general foreman, moved from Cheyenne to the headquarters at Chugwater, and the economy drive was under way. Over the years the labor and management expenses were reduced by half.

The Cheyenne office was virtually bankrupt when Clay arrived. Unable to get satisfactory help from the Cheyenne bank, Clay borrowed seventy-five thousand dollars from Lyman Gage, of the First National Bank of Chicago, to cover the operation of the ranch for the summer. With support from the home office the ranching operation was also under way.[36] "The open range was passing . . . but for years the Swan Company considered itself a range company, till

[34] Clay, *My Life on the Range*, 203.
[35] *Ibid.*, 207.
[36] *Ibid.*, 207–10.

gradually it was left alone a solitary ship surrounded by rocks and quicksand in the form of small ranchmen, sheepmen, and dry farmers."[37]

With the help of Al Bowie, Clay began to make changes. The ranches were rented, the tenants being paid so much a ton for the hay they stacked and the tenants in turn feeding out the hay through the winter. The major effort was to preserve the herds by consolidating them on certain ranches during the winter months for feed and shelter. These practices were the results of what had been learned in the tragic winter of 1886–87. Clay wrote: "As we raised hay and improved our pastures we began weaning calves, feeding the cows and heifers, while away on the plains in Bates' Hole . . . our steers took their chances."[38]

Clay's policy was actually a combination of the recommendations of Johnston and Tait. As the herd began to take some sort of shape, the company gradually added a few cattle in the better years. A Swan ranch hand explained that Clay's theory "was to buy cattle cheap and sell them high."[39] Clay, in a brief paragraph, paints the scope of his eight years as manager of the Swan Company:

> While it does not take long to write the account of those changes, it was a great task to reorganize the machinery of the ranch work, cut down the cattle outfits . . . and look after the feeding of twelve to fifteen thousand head of cattle in pasture. As the work contracted we had to face blackleg and destruction by wolves among our calves, and more or less mange appeared among the cattle. Most of our neighbors sold out and left us. Sheep trespassers on our plains lands were hard to handle and we had a continual fight on

[37] *Ibid.*, 204.
[38] *Ibid.*, 216.

our hands. . . . To improve the herd and keep it up to standard we bought a good many purebred bulls. . . . We began
spaying 10 to 15 per cent of our yearling heifers before
turning them out on the pasture. In this way we got quit of
the delicate, light-boned tail-end of our female herd.[40]

The management of the ranches in America was left entirely to Clay. He operated, in most instances, without the
need for prior approval from the home office. He took both
the blame and the credit, and while more of the former
than of the latter was forthcoming, the home board for most
of the Clay reign was agreeable to his program. Toward
the end of his managership, however, its members became
restless and aggressive.[41] Not all the shareholders were as
sure of Clay as was the board. At the annual meeting in
1890 at least two shareholders expressed their doubts about
having one man again so completely in charge of the
American operations. They questioned the advisability of
having the same man as both cattle salesman for the company and manager.[42]

Clay was kept on as manager on a yearly basis until June,
1896, when he was dismissed. No one, not even Clay, was
sure about the reason for his dismissal. The board put it in
nice terms:

> The changes in the American management referred to
> in the Report are being carried out. The Directors are sever-
> ing their connection with Mr. Clay. That had become neces-

[39] A. S. ("Bud") Gillespie, "The Swan Land and Cattle Company"
(manuscript), Wyoming State Department of History and Archives,
Cheyenne.

[40] Clay, *My Life on the Range*, 216–17.

[41] *Ibid.*, 213 and 220.

[42] "Seventh Annual General Meeting," March 18, 1890.

sary on account of his own private business, and they parted with him on friendly terms.[43]

This was not quite the way Clay saw it. "This was a sugar-coated pill because in plain language I was 'fired.' " He also implies that Finlay Dun was instrumental in his removal.[44] But Clay thought only a little more highly of Finlay Dun than Lawson did. Clay's career with the Swan Company did not end in 1896, however, for he returned about fifteen years later as head of the American executive committee.

While John Clay was struggling to develop the Swan ranches into a paying proposition, the board was making every effort to improve the financial affairs of the company. They were heavily in debt from debentures, unpaid calls on shares, and the loss of capital as represented by the cattle. The company's finances were the most important matter with which the shareholders had to deal at the sixth annual general meeting. The company held a bank over-draft of some twenty-six thousand pounds and the bankers insisted on "repayment or security." The members of the board and a few other shareholders provided the necessary security by giving the bank their personal guarantee until December, 1891. The board was quick to point out that this was not a satisfactory arrangement because it placed too great a responsibility on the board and left affairs too much in its hands.[45]

Although in serious financial trouble, the company did not really consider winding up its affairs. To go into forced liquidation would have meant a great sacrifice of property. A special extraordinary general meeting resulted in this

[43] "Thirteenth Annual General Meeting," March 17, 1896.
[44] Clay, *My Life on the Range*, 219.
[45] "Sixth Annual General Meeting," March 26, 1889.

resolution: "That the Company shall not be dissolved and wound up."[46]

Over the next two years the board began to take steps to find out what the actual assets were. A draft agenda for a directors' meeting for September 29, 1891, did include an "adjustment of evaluation of herds and lands and cutting down of capital" in the amount of $1,525,445.[47]

John Guthrie Watson of LaMars, Iowa, was commissioned by the board to report on the Swan property for the purpose of determining the financial assets of the company. The company considered arranging for a loan of one hundred thousand pounds with the Scottish American Investment Company.[48]

Watson's report valued the property as follows:

I. Value of patented lands, 22,000 acres at $10	$ 220,000
II. Value of Union Pacific lands, (6 contracts); doubted that the lands could be sold for the suggested price of (but could not be realized immediately)	355,000
III. Cattle: an estimated 45,000 head (should be no problem in selling the cattle)	640,000 net
IV. Income from the cattle had averaged for the past three years (1888, 1889, 1890)	133,445

[46] "Extraordinary General Meeting," March 26, 1889.
[47] "Draft Agenda for Directors' Meeting for September 29, 1891."
[48] "Printed Notice, Swan Land and Cattle Company, Limited" (stating a proposal of borrowing £100,000 by giving all their land and cattle as mortgage security).

V. Horses: 450 at $30 per head; 140 at $20 per head	16,380
VI. Improvements on all ranches	12,000
VII. Implements and equipment	4,500
	$ 1,381,325[49]

Fraser drafted a mortgage contract with the Scottish American Investment Company, dated November 1, 1891, in the amount of one hundred thousand pounds for ten years, at 6 per cent a year, by the issuance of bonds. The bonds could be redeemed at par, plus interest, any time after November 1, 1896.[50] In December, 1891, Swift and Campbell reported to William John Menzies, of the Scottish American Investment Company, on the lands and cattle held by the company and advised him about their use as security for a loan. The lands, they said, could be used as real-estate security, and the cattle as chattel security.[51] Within less than three weeks the company had decided that the loan was not necessary and that it could better handle the financial arrangements by a reduction of capital and an issuance of debentures to meet its various debts.

A letter to the shareholders stated the proposed changes in sufficient detail that the necessary decisions could be made at the annual meeting.[52] For this purpose copies of all resolutions to be voted on were included in the letter. The capital of the company was reduced from £900,000,

[49] John Guthrie Watson, *Report upon the Property of the Swan Land and Cattle Company, Limited* (printed), November 23, 1891.
[50] Contract, "Scottish American Investment Company, Limited" (draft copy), November 1, 1891.
[51] "Report, Swift & Campbell to Wm. John Menzies of the Scottish American Investment Company," Chicago, December 21, 1891.
[52] "Letter to Shareholders," February 24, 1892.

divided into 15,000 preference shares of £10 each and 75,-000 ordinary shares of £10 each, to £300,000, divided into 15,000 £10 preference shares and 75,000 £2 ordinary shares. The amount of the ordinary shares which were fully paid was reduced from £750,000 to £150,000 by canceling £8 a share as "lost and unrepresented by available assets."[53] The shareholders authorized the raising of £60,000 on 6 per cent debentures to pay off the bank debt and an additional £15,000 to provide necessary working capital for the company. The total amount of the debenture loan was set at £75,000, in £100 debentures issued at £95 and redeemable by annual drawings at par (£100) beginning December 31, 1895.[54] Only £25,000 of the debenture capital (£60,-000) had been raised at the time the shareholders met, and the chairman asked the shareholders to contribute the remaining £35,000 to avoid going into liquidation.

Great sacrifices had been made in both Wyoming and Edinburgh. At the ranch it was necessary to "dip a little freely into the herd to make ends meet."[55] The company decided to relinquish the Carbon County railroad lands since "everybody with a flock of sheep or a bunch of cattle ranged over them" and the company got more headaches from court battles against trespassers than it did value from the use of the land. Clay concluded, "Those financial changes, the call up of subscribed capital, thus paying debentures and bank debts, abandoning the above lands, the cutting of expenses, left us on this side in a much easier position."[56] However, conditions were only temporarily relieved in Edinburgh. Most of the financial progress had

[53] "Notice of Meeting to Shareholders," March 11, 1892.
[54] "Ninth Annual General Meeting," March 22, 1892.
[55] Clay, *My Life on the Range*, 218.
[56] *Ibid.*, 218–19.

been made by the great financial sacrifice of the ordinary shareholder. The cumulative preference shares and debenture loans, many of which were in arrears, continued to use up the profit of the company, making working capital difficult to produce and dividends on ordinary shares nearly impossible.

Although the years between 1888 and 1896 were not the best years for livestock in Wyoming, the company did manage to make a fair showing. There were periods of drought, periods of too much rain for the grass to cure, and some severe winters. In the winter of 1893–94, the company had to provide feed and shelter for some 10,000 head. The gains were not enough to remove the burden of debt. In 1892 the shareholders passed a resolution to issue three fully paid preference shares for each holder of ten in order to wipe out the cumulative arrears of preference dividends of some £17,640.[57]

Two years later the company decided on a reduction-of-capital scheme. It became necessary to cancel the preference shares and redeem the 6 per cent debentures because the payments on these two financial obligations were using up the profits. According to an act of 1867, a company had to petition the court for a reduction of capital and add the word "reduced" to its name.[58] Debenture holders were notified that all debentures were to be paid off on June 30, 1898.[59] At an extraordinary general meeting held on February 22, 1898, the shareholders passed two resolutions.

[57] "Report by Directors to the Twelfth Annual Meeting," March 12, 1895.
[58] "Petition of the Swan Land and Cattle Company, Limited, and Reduced for Confirmation of Reduction of Capital. To Lords of Council and Sessions, First Division," March 16, 1898.
[59] "Intimation to Debenture-Holders," December 30, 1897.

The first was to increase the capital of the company to £400,000 by the creation of 10,000 new £10 shares with a fixed cumulative preferential dividend of 5 per cent a year. The second would reduce the company's capital from £400,000, to £250,000, divided into 75,000 ordinary shares of £2 each, fully paid, and 10,000 5 per cent preference shares of £10. To the holders of the 7,500 5 per cent preference shares the amount of their paid-up capital was returned, and the other 7,500, which were never issued, were canceled.[60] The company confirmed the latter resolution at an extraordinary general meeting on March 15, 1898, and the court confirmed the reduction on May 12, 1898.[61]

The problems confronting the Swan Company were not unique but common to the entire cattle industry of the western plains. The winter of 1886–87 and the earlier loose control of the board had finally stirred the Scottish shareholders to action. The company was not reaping the anticipated profit, but to the shareholders the possibility of losing the capital they had already invested was of even graver concern. The decision to sacrifice 80 per cent of the investment of the ordinary shareholder took not only great courage but also considerable faith. That faith, for the present, was placed in the hands of such men as Alexander McNab and John Clay, who were expected to lead the company, one at home and the other in America, out of its financial distress.

It was a time of waiting both for the Swan Company and for the cattle industry as a whole. Prosperity was no longer just around the corner. It was somewhere over the far horizon—but it was still there.

[60] "Notice of Extraordinary General Meeting," February 22, 1898.
[61] Charles B. Logan, "Report to the Lords of the First Division of the Court of Sessions," May 12, 1898.

CHAPTER VI

Land and Sheep

As THE nineteenth century drew to a close, America became increasingly concerned about the exploitation of the public domain by corporate enterprise. With the founding of the British-American cattle companies in the boom years of 1882 and 1883, the demand to preserve the land for the benefit of the settler steadily increased. It was not, however, until the administration of President Grover Cleveland that much was accomplished. By presidential proclamation the "free grassers" were driven off the Cherokee Strip and the Indian reservations in the Southwest. Portions of the Indian Territory had been sold as grazing interests to several foreign companies. Also southwestern cattlemen, notably the members of the Cherokee Strip Livestock Association, had negotiated with the Indians for virtually free use of the land. Not only did the President's proclamation halt such practices but also it caused the market to be flooded with poor, unfinished beef in 1885, when the cattle on the Indian lands were forced onto the market.[1]

While the President took immediate action to prevent

misuse of the Indian lands, it remained for Congress to do something about the public domain. In 1885 and again in 1886 the House of Representatives considered bills restricting alien ownership of lands in the territories. The House Committee on Public Lands submitted a bill in July, 1886, which provided that no foreigner, resident or nonresident alien, or corporation in which 10 per cent of the stock was held by aliens could hold or acquire lands in the United States. In reporting the bill, Representative Lewis E. Payson of Illinois explained that the committee was

> thoroughly committed to the policy of so adjusting and administering our public land system that the agricultural lands of the nation shall be parted with, without cost, to be held in small tracts by actual settlers only, for the purpose of cultivation by the owner, securing thereby the thrift of the citizen and economy in his management which ownership always stimulates.[2]

The Senate submitted its own bill prohibiting alien ownership of lands, a more comprehensive measure than that of the House. A compromise was not effected until the next session, and President Cleveland signed the bill March 3, 1887.

As finally passed, the bill prohibited all aliens and for-

---

[1] For a thorough discussion of the issue of a alien ownership of public lands see Jackson, *The Enterprising Scot*, 101–13; Roger V. Clements, "British Investment and American Legislative Restrictions in the Trans-Mississippi West, 1880–1900," *Mississippi Valley Historical Review*, Vol. XLII (September, 1955), 207–28. For the Indian land controversy, see Dale, *Cow Country*, 202–11; and Dale, *The Range Cattle Industry*, 106–107. Unless otherwise indicated, all information in this chapter is taken from the Swan files of the WRCIS.

[2] U.S. Congress, House, *Report of the House Committee on Public Lands on the Ownership of Real Estate in the Territories by Foreigners*, 49th Cong., 1st sess., 1886, *House Report No. 3455*, 1.

eign corporations in which more than 20 per cent of the stock was held by foreigners from holding real estate in the territories. No corporations organized for the construction or operation of canals, railroads, or turnpikes could hold in excess of five thousand acres more than was necessary to operate such a business.[3] The Swan Company's titles were not affected by the new law except for those lands to which title might be questionable or not yet fully secured.

The open range created a problem of ownership. Unless secured by title, the land was public land, open to everyone. Ownership was usually a matter of possession, and squatters' rights were usually recognized. Cattlemen strung barbed-wire fences to protect not only their titled lands but also those that they felt rightfully belonged to them by occupancy. Often millions of acres of public lands were fenced off from settlement, and as the pioneer farmer moved onto the plains, he encountered a barbed-wire barricade. In 1883, George W. Fairfield, a deputy United States surveyor in northwestern Nebraska, reported that the whole country was occupied and run by large cattle companies. Wire fences surrounded creeks and meadows to keep others out. Posted at intervals along the fences were signs with the unmistakable warning to the trespasser and fence cutter: "The son of a bitch who opens the fence had better look out for his scalp."[4]

From 1882 until 1887 the struggle between cattlemen and homesteaders over the fencing of the public domain

[3] U.S. *Statutes at Large*, Vol. XXIV (1886–87), "An Act to Restrict the Ownership of Real Estate in the Territories to American Citizens, and so Forth," March 3, 1887, 476–77.

[4] U.S. Congress, Senate, *Report of the Commissioner of the General Land Office on the Unauthorized Fencing of the Public Lands*, 48th Cong., 1st sess., 1883, *Sen. Ex. Doc. No. 127*, Part 2.

raged on the plains and in the halls of Congress. From time to time Alexander Swan, his partners, and friends became involved in the struggle. Swan entered the contest early in 1883, when he brought suit for $960 against "old man Odder," who had allegedly cut down several miles of fence belonging to Swan.[5]

The same account announced the issuance of an order to the United States district attorney directing him to prosecute all parties who had fenced in the public domain. There are sufficient entries of cases to prove that the government officer did not shrink from his duty.

The chancery records of the District Court of Laramie County lists one suit against Swan et al. and suits against owners of land later acquired by the company. Only one of the cases is complete: *The United States of America* v. *Hiram B. Kelly,* entered December 22, 1883. The bill of complaint, served on January 5, 1884, accused Kelly of surveying and dividing and subdividing land into townships, sections, and quarter sections. It was further alleged that he had "wrongfully and unlawfully enclosed a part thereof, to-wit: about Thirty-Two Thousand acres with fences composed chiefly of barbed wire, in to several enclosures, and is now keeping said enclosures."[6]

The other cases vary only in amount of damages claimed and location of fences. Occasionally notices of the cases appeared in the local press and the court docket, but no decisions were recorded. The practice was to delay court action until the fences could be removed or the enclosed land was purchased; then the cases were allowed to drop.

[5] *Carbon County Journal,* January 13, 1883.
[6] *United States of America* v. *Hiram B. Kelly,* Chancery Records, No. 1–70, District Court of Laramie County, Cheyenne, Territory of Wyoming, 1883–86.

Two years after the cases were entered on the docket, the *Carbon County Journal* was to announce that "the notorious Swan Fence case came up for argument Tuesday on demurr Attorney Woolworth, of Omaha, and Corlett, of this city representing the defendants and U.S. District Attorney Riner the government. The matter was taken under advisement by the Court."[7]

Although the courts were reluctant to make decisions in many fence cases, the desired effect was nevertheless accomplished. According to the local newspaper, some of the large cattle companies had already begun removing their fences as a "result of the war like attitude of the government in the matter of fencing the public domain."[8] In regard to the particular case in point, the paper stated that the "Swan Land and Cattle Company has already removed about forty miles of its barbed wire barriers, throwing open Sabile [*sic*] and Chugwater Creeks to the cattle at large."[9] This action, the paper believed, would "be followed by many more of the large companies as preparations by the government are for a thorough raid upon them."[10]

It was not government action, however, which brought down the fences. Before the laws of man could remove the evil, the laws of nature did. Nothing hastened the removal of fences as much as the winter of 1886–87. Fences kept the cattle from drifting with the storms and finding natural shelter, and each barbed-wire fence became a dead line for the herds. When the melting snows uncovered the carcasses lined up along each fence, the fences came down.

Fortunately for the Swan herds, many of their fences

[7] *Carbon County Journal*, January 3, 1885.
[8] *Ibid.*, September 27, 1884.
[9] *Ibid.*
[10] *Ibid.*

were down before the storms of 1886–87. The Swan Company was not named as one of the major violators of the law against fencing the public domain or as an illegal holder of public lands. The company's image was little damaged by its alien status although it was troubled by the protests against foreign ownership. Cattle had dominated the interest of the company during the early years, but as the cattle industry became less profitable and less certain, land became the more positive asset. While land was of greater value, however, it was also a greater problem. With livestock it was possible in a good year to sell out and realize an immediate profit. With land, especially of uncertain and diverse value, such sudden liquidation was impossible. Thus the attention of the company shifted from cattle to land.

Initially the company was interested in holding land in order to control the water. The law of the range gave a man all the land his water rights controlled. The consolidation of these holdings had been greatly benefited by the acquisition of the Kelly and Whitcomb properties in 1884. These lands plus a few thousand acres of desert lands on which the company held patents would eventually comprise the Chugwater, or Eastern Division. They were, of course, the more valuable lands, but their use was greatly hindered by the arrival of the dry farmer.[11] On the west lay the Laramie Plains, and in 1884 an ambitious Alexander Swan began a campaign for control of a large portion of them.

In the spring of 1884 the Union Pacific Railroad was offering land in Wyoming for $1.25 to $1.50 an acre. West

[11] "Report by the Directors to the Second Annual Meeting," March 11, 1885. From H. B. Kelly, 3,200 acres; from E. W. Whitcomb, 1,543 acres; owned in fee simple 14,454 acres; and claimed under the Desert Act, 27,781 acres.

of the mountains 135,000 acres had already been sold. Swan wanted 30,000 to 40,000 acres of these lands for the company, but they had been sold to a syndicate while Swan was in Scotland. Swan believed that the company was compelled to buy at least 200,000 acres west to the Carbon County line to prevent them from falling into the hands of speculators. Swan had already offered $1.00 an acre for the railroad land and thought it could be bought for no more than $1.50 an acre.[12] In brief, he considered it necessary to buy the lands not only for the use of the range but also to prevent speculation on them. There can be no doubt that Swan believed that the lands, if bought at a low price, would greatly add to the value of the company.[13]

The board was not long in approving Swan's preliminary offers to the railroad. By the middle of June he had permission to purchase four to five hundred thousand acres of land.[14] After nearly two weeks of unceasing work, Swan was able to report that he had reached a provisional agreement with the railroad to purchase an aggregate of nearly a half million acres in various tracts at an average cost not to exceed sixty-five cents an acre. Approval was necessary by the railroad board at Boston before it could conclude the contract, but no changes were expected, and Swan believed that the land would be worth at least two million dollars in the future.[15]

Swan had considered himself "bold" when he offered the low price of fifty cents an acre. He became somewhat self-congratulatory once the deal was accepted: "I have

[12] A. H. Swan to William S. Fraser, May 31, 1884.
[13] *Ibid.*, June 18, 1884.
[14] *Ibid.*
[15] *Ibid.*, June 27, 1884.

secured the land on the terms proposed by myself as a consideration due to myself for many favors heretofore extended to the Railway officials."[16] As the final terms were arranged, it became clear that fears Swan had expressed about speculations were well founded. The syndicate had paid $1.00 an acre for lands, 5,400 acres of which it later sold to the company at $1.50 an acre. Swan believed the syndicate purchase was a "godsend" since it gave him a bargaining lever. He lowered the price from $0.80 to $0.50 by threatening to move to Mexico. Personally, Swan was elated over the terms and had every right to be. "I feel very good over this and am sure yourself and the whole Board will rejoice with me."[17]

The lands, comprising an area about eighty miles long and twenty miles wide, lying in alternate sections along the north side of the Union Pacific tracks, contained 549,423 acres and cost $460,900.[18] The company now had over 600,000 acres of land, acquired or in process, at an average cost of $1.54 an acre. With the alternate government sections, this gave the company well over a million acres of grazing lands. The railroad sections cost them $0.63 an acre but were entered in the books at $0.84 an acre, that price including the interest on the unpaid balance.[19]

It would be difficult to deny that Swan had made a very good bargain. It also appeared that he had an excellent reputation with the railroad officials and that they were, for reasons not known, indebted to Swan. Good as the bargain

[16] *Ibid.*, July 12, 1884.

[17] *Ibid.*

[18] "Report by the Directors to Second Annual General Meeting," March 11, 1885.

[19] *Ibid.*

was, the lands became a source of annual anxiety, first, about how valid the contract was, and second, how best to realize a return from them.

The original contract was made between Alexander Swan and the Union Pacific Railroad Company. Swan, before going on to Scotland in the spring of 1886, stopped in Boston to talk with Mr. Frederick L. Ames, trustee for the railroad lands. What the Swan Company wanted was a confirmation by the Union Pacific Railway Company of Swan's contract with the railroad. Ames did not feel that he could make such a written confirmation, but he told Swan that he could assure the board of the validity of the contract.[20]

Later in the month, at the 1886 annual meeting, Swan assured the shareholders that the railroad lands could be sold for double or triple their cost. Therefore, with the threat of the alien bill hanging over the title to the lands, the directors felt it desirable to raise the necessary money —sixty thousand pounds—to make the purchase and to get an inalienable title to them. At an extraordinary meeting the shareholders increased the capital of the company to nine hundred thousand pounds by the creation of fifteen thousand pounds in new preference shares of 10 pounds each.[21]

The problems created by these shares and the use to which the capital was put have already been discussed. It is sufficient to say here that during the rest of the century the directors were concerned about the precise location and value of and the nature of the title to all their lands. The

[20] "Swan's Statement to Board of Directors—Re Ames," Director's Minute, March 4, 1886.
[21] "Report of the Third Annual General Meeting," March 12, 1886.

correspondence between the offices in Cheyenne and Edinburgh is full of questions over titles, requests for additional information, and the deteriorating land patents. The company even asked its American attorneys, Swift and Campbell, to examine the possibility of a suit against Swan for the failure of some of the titles and proofs to stand legal tests.

As mentioned earlier, the 1886 capital increase was not used to pay for the railroad lands as intended; instead an arrangement was made with the railroad whereby the company would make no payment on the principal for five years but would pay the interest on the unpaid balance at the rate of 6 per cent a year.[22] If the company had made enough profit from its cattle, as it had fully expected to do, to pay off the land indebtedness, then the land would have been an asset. However, after the disaster of 1886–87, it did not appear that land, especially that on the plains, was of material value to the company. With the great depletion of cattle and considerable grazing, the company did not suffer greatly from overstocking throughout the rest of the century. In the light of these developments, the railroad land was certainly worth no more than what they had paid for it. Swan had guessed right but with the wrong results. Cattle formed the key to the control of the range and the value of the land. Under the existing circumstances the depreciation in the value of cattle resulted in a similar reduction in land values. By July, 1887, the company held a total of 577,120 acres, with title to an additional 17,898 still incomplete, and had relinquished title to 11,029 acres.[23] By then the company had become particularly concerned about its lands. The killing winter and the alien act had

[22] "Dun Reports," June 8, 1887.
[23] See Appendix C.

made them acutely aware of this heretofore unrealized asset.

By 1891 low cattle prices, the arrival of sheepmen and dry farmers, a debenture debt, and dividends in arrears had placed the company in financial difficulty. The arrangement with the railroad for payment on the lands would expire the same year. Thus the company was confronted with a major problem. It could relinquish its railroad lands, use the lands as collateral on a loan, or reorganize the company. As already indicated, the company favored reorganization, but it also considered the other alternatives.

Throughout 1891 the board explored all the possibilities of its railroad lands. Its members wanted to abandon the less valuable and retain the more valuable. That, however, was not possible. The land was held under two major contracts, one for 286,473.08 acres, the other for 179,305.48 acres, and the company could abandon either of them or both but could not pick certain tracts under either contract.[24] Swift and Campbell thought it desirable to retain all the land, but in the fall of 1891, Clay asked the board to consider relinquishing the Carbon County land.[25]

The following spring, while the board was considering a loan from the Scottish American Mortgage Company, William John Menzies, of that firm, was informed by Swift and Campbell that the lands must be included in any mortgage and that the cattle could not be sold to pay for the land.[26] Throughout the negotiations for the loan Swift and Campbell stuck to their original advice to keep all the lands and somehow raise sufficient money to pay off all of the

[24] Swift and Campbell to John Clay, May 15, 1891.
[25] "Draft Agenda for Director's Meeting," September 29, 1891 (copy of cable from Clay).
[26] Swift and Campbell to William John Menzies, February 1, 1892.

indebtedness.[27] However, the company chose to give up the 283,226 acres in Carbon County and authorized a debenture loan to pay for the remainder. Final payment was made in December, 1894.[28] For the rest of the century the board maintained the hope that its cattle would provide enough revenue to pay the debenture interest and also dividends on the shares. The board members were constantly alert for opportunities to sell portions of their land, but such opportunities did not occur. Agricultural prices were low, and the land was a drug on the market.

In 1905, discouraged by the cattle market and the uncertainty of the weather, the directors decided to introduce sheep to their ranges.[29] Sheep brought about a major change in the ranching operation. According to John Clay: "The advent of the sheep was the beginning of the end of the range business so far as the Swan Company was concerned." The open range was gone. "Its death rattle echoed over its broad acres in three words, 'the dry farmer.' "[30] By 1909 the dry farmer had settled on the available lands, thrown up his fences, chased, dogged, and stolen cattle, and generally so interfered with ranching that the directors decided to sell all the cattle and buy more sheep. Sheep replaced cattle because it was possible to herd sheep flocks on obstructed ranges; it was not possible to herd cattle in such fashion. But sheep fared no better in the market place than had cattle. It was also decided that all acreage not

[27] Swift to William John Menzies, February 4, 1892.

[28] "The Tenth Annual General Meeting," March 21, 1893; "Report of Directors to the Tenth Annual General Meeting," March 22, 1893; "Report of Directors to the Twelfth Annual General Meeting," March 12, 1895.

[29] "The Twenty-third Annual General Meeting," March 5, 1906.

[30] Clay, *My Life on the Range*, 221.

necessary for grazing sheep would be sold. Wool prices were so low that the entire 1910 clip of 555,558 pounds was sent to a Boston firm to be disposed of when the price increased.[31] The sheep business went into a major depression about 1911 and did not make a significant recovery until the outbreak of World War I.

When the directors decided to sell the cattle and increase the sheep, they also decided to obtain a reliable appraisal and evaluation of the land. The company had never had reliable working information about the location of its lands, the most prosperous arrangement of them, or the return to expect from them. As long as the range was open, such information had not been vital. Now, however, with the range filled with farmers and grazing obstructed, a precise knowledge of how best to use the range, what lands to dispose of, and what to retain was imperative. George Forman and Company, a Chicago surveying and soil firm, was employed to make a detailed survey and evaluation of the company's lands. The Forman report was submitted to the directors in 1911 and 1912. The property was appraised by sections and by "ranches"; the soil, water, climate, and future use of the land were examined and reported.

The report became the plan for the future realization of the property, but it was not yet available when the shareholders met in March, 1911. The ordinary shareholder who had sacrificed 8 pounds of the original 10 pounds invested in the company and who had not received a dividend since, was eager for some return on his capital. One shareholder —who undoubtedly spoke for many—was of the opinion that "selling at $5.00 or $10.00 per acre today was as valuable to the shareholder as $10.00 or $20.00 ten year

[31] *Letter to Shareholders* (printed), May 31, 1910.

hence."[32] The directors, however, refused to make any decisions about the disposal of the property until the Forman report was received.[33]

The first volume of the Forman report, submitted April 1, 1911, covered the plains section. For the time being, it concluded, the primary use of the plains was grazing. Altogether the firm comprised thirty-one ranches in the plains section, varying in size from 2,392 acres to 21,452 acres, averaging about 8,365 acres a ranch. The average value of the land was $3.77 an acre. The appraisal was accompanied by a map of the physiographic features, drainage, water supply, roads, fences, improvements, grades of lands, all located by sections. The report concluded that the subdivision of the land into ranches would be the best method of disposing of the land.[34]

The report on the lands lying north of the plains section was submitted on December 11, 1911. These lands consisted of isolated areas along Sheep Creek, Little Medicine Creek, Little Medicine River, and the Bates Hole country. The land, soil, and climate were nearly the same as the plains, but the land consisted of seven "ranches" bought by the company, and each was appraised separately. Collectively they amounted to 2,716.33 acres at about $7.00 an acre, at a total of $19,291.98. The Bates Hole land was appraised at $12.00 an acre, the 49 Ranch and the ranch

[32] "The Twenty-eighth Annual General Meeting," March 27, 1911.

[33] *Ibid.* See also *Letter from Martin, Currie & Co., C. A. To Chairman* (printed), June 7, 1910, a copy of which was sent to all shareholders; and the director's reply in *Letter to the Shareholders* (printed), June 23, 1910.

[34] *Report and Appraisal of Lands in Albany and Carbon Counties, Wyo., Belonging to the Swan Land and Cattle Company, Limited, of Edinburgh, Scotland,* by George M. Forman and Company, Chicago, Illinois. Hereafter cited as *Forman Report.*

at "42 mile crossing" at $8.00 an acre, and the others in varying amounts down to $5.00 an acre.[35]

The Elk Mountain lands, 7,837 acres lying in the east-central portion of Carbon County, were so remote from the rest of the company's property that Forman appraised them at $2.90 an acre and recommended disposing of them as soon as possible. The lands were regarded as valueless for agriculture and were difficult to reach. The only possible reason for retaining them would be the probable coal deposits they held.[36]

The lands in the eastern division were more difficult to obtain information on, and that report was not submitted until February 15, 1912. The eastern division, in the Chugwater, Sybille, and Platte river valleys totaled 38,671 acres. Of these, 28,711 acres were bottom lands with some 3,300 irrigated acres and 30,592 acres cultivated dry.

The lands, all valley sections, had been acquired by the company to control water rights. Under the open-range system the company had enjoyed the use of all the lands controlled by their water. With the advent of the dry farmer that was no longer true. Since John Clay's years of management the lands had been used to provide hay and winter shelter for the herds and flocks, but it was becoming increasingly difficult to drive the herds from the plains division to the Chugwater division. In this respect the use of the lands had lessened. That did not necessarily mean that their value had declined. On the contrary, the Forman report held that the company owned some of the best agricultural land in the state. The value of these lands would

---

[35] *Ibid.*

[36] *Report on The Elk Mountain Lands, Carbon County, Wyo.* (separate folder), December 19, 1911. *Forman Report.*

be greatly enhanced by sufficient water for irrigation, and the company was advised to acquire and maintain as many water rights as possible.

In southwestern Wyoming for every acre that could be irrigated two could be cultivated dry and ten could be grazed. "The future use of the valley lands depends almost entirely on agricultural development and the latter on improved systems of irrigation."[37] Forman believed that with irrigation much of the company's lands could be made as productive as any in southwestern Wyoming. Therefore this portion of the report paid special attention to irrigation prospects.

So far as company land was concerned, there were in all six different irrigation possibilities. Five of these were proposed reservoirs on company property; the sixth, a government project in Goshen Hole.

Before the report was submitted, irrigation had utilized only the summer flow of water in the various streams, an oftentimes irregular and uncontrollable practice. To establish an irrigation system, reservoirs would have to be built to hold the winter flow of water from the snows and spring thaws.

The company's engineer, Frank M. Johnson, had suggested sites for four reservoirs on the company's property. The Shepard Reservoir, located about thirty miles south of Chugwater, would cost $83,107.50, or about $42.94 for each acre of irrigated land. Forman advised selling the land and the water rights. The A. L. Reservoir, about a mile and one-half west of the A. L. Ranch, would provide water for about six hundred acres of A. L. land and other irrigable land for

[37] *Report and Appraisal of Lands in Platte, Goshen, Laramie and Albany Counties, Wyoming, and Scotts Bluff County, Nebraska.*

nine or ten miles down Chugwater Creek, at a cost of $36.86 for each acre of irrigated land. Forman doubted the reservoir would be practical at that price and said that unless the cost could be reduced to $25.00 or $30.00 they should not build. About ten miles north of Chugwater on Richard Creek was another proposed site; however, the company did not own the land, and the cost would be $40.86 for each acre without the land. This site was not feasible.

On the M Bar Ranch, nine miles north of Chugwater, was another site. This one might well prove profitable if enough water came down the Chugwater to fill the reservoir. It would require a dam 2,269 feet long and 81 feet high. The reservoir would cover 647 acres. However, the dam would have to be faced on the pressure side. A rip-rap facing would cost $283,996.00 or $34.78 for each acre of land irrigated; a concrete facing could be added for $240,200.00 or $26.70 for each acre of irrigated land. About 9,000 acres could be irrigated if there was enough water.

The Peters Ranch reservoirs were the only two the company owned at the time. They provided the irrigation for both the Wyoming and the Nebraska sections of the Peters Ranch, but the water supply was not adequate to warrant an enlargement of the operation.

The final prospect in the eastern division was the government's proposed Goshen Hole irrigation project. A dam on the Platte River would provide the reservoir. The only lands of the company which could be watered from the government dam were portions of the T. H. and Peters ranches, both of which were already partly irrigated. Water from the government ditch would cost thirty to forty dollars an acre, and so it was not feasible for the company to consider this solution.[38]

On the Laramie Plains there was also a possibility of irrigation. There were only two practical projects: one, a dam on Sheep Creek and an enlargement of Badger Lake; the other, a reservoir at Lake Ione on the Laramie River near the Shearing Pens Ranch. The construction of the first, along with supply canals, trunk laterals, and distributing ditches, would cost $266,453, or about $18.38 for each acre of land irrigated. If the project was carried out, about 14,500 acres could be irrigated. Including construction and interest on the money and allowing $5.00 for unirrigated land adjacent to the project, the company could expect a profit of no less than $88,600. The Lake Ione reservoir would irrigate 9,000 acres at an average cost of $11.11 an acre, and the company should realize a profit of no less than $150,000.[39]

The Forman report subdivided the lands into ninety different ranches, forty on the plains and fifty on the Chugwater division. The plains ranches averaged 8,365 acres in size and were appraised at $3.77 an acre; the Chugwater division ranches averaged 710 acres at $13.00 an acre.

In 1893 the board had appraised its lands at $.50 an acre for railroad lands which were of value only for grazing, and $18.00 an acre for all the freehold lands that could be used for agriculture. Forman's appraisal of 1912 listed them in somewhat different categories, but generally the plains sections were the railroad lands and the freehold lands were the remaining ones.

A recapitulation of value covering the whole of the company's lands showed the following figures:

Location	Acres	Value
Plains section	259,315.89	$ 979,716.65
Sheep Creek and Little		
Medicine lands	2,716.33	19,291.98
Elk Mountain lands	7,837.11	19,671.97
Valley sections	38,671.90	484,834.60
	308,541.23	$1,503,515.20[40]

The board was advised to hold off the market all the lands that might be irrigated until the irrigation schemes could be thoroughly investigated and to follow the suggested subdivision into ranches, so that the poor land could be sold with the good.[41]

When the shareholders met in March, 1912, they were presented with the broad outlines of the Forman report—and with the hope that the company could soon begin to realize a return from the land.[42] The Forman recommendations were seriously followed for the next several years. Land sales were slow, and only a few outlying areas were disposed of. A dam was begun on the M Bar Ranch in 1915, but the project was abandoned two years later after tests indicated that the soil around the dam would not hold and construction proved too expensive.[43]

By 1914 the government lands in Goshen Hole were being rapidly settled, increasing the value of company land

[40] *Forman Report*, Vol. 2, 455.
[41] *Ibid.*, 457–59.
[42] "Twenty-ninth Annual General Meeting," March 28, 1912.
[43] "Thirty-first Annual General Meeting," March 10, 1914.

in that area.[44] Within a year so much of the land in Goshen Hole had been taken up by dry farmers that the area was no longer of value as a winter range. The chairman of the Scottish board, J. C. Johnston, who had visited the ranges in the spring of 1915, announced that when the public lands around the government irrigation project in Goshen Hole opened up it would "be good-bye so far as open grazing is concerned to our company in that region."[45]

On the plains the entire operation had been reorganized. Winter pens had been built, steel bins set up for grain storage, and irrigation pushed wherever possible to provide more hay and grain. Dry farmers had moved onto the plains and settled the state lands and also public lands that the company had always used. The number of sheep therefore had to be reduced. Nevertheless, all signs pointed to a revival in real estate, and the company could soon expect some return on the land.[46]

John Clay and Company was commissioned by the board to handle all sales of lands in the Goshen Hole area, and power of attorney was given to the Wyoming Trust and Savings Bank of Cheyenne to transfer lands sold by the company. The disposal of lands in the eastern division was in the hands of the American executive committee.[47] Regardless of the signs of hope expressed by both Clay and Johnston, however, the company did not make any progress

[44] "Minute of Meeting of Directors," May 8, 1914; "Minute of Meeting," July 17, 1914.
[45] "Report by Mr. J. C. Johnston to Directors of the Swan Land and Cattle Company, Ltd., upon his visit to the Company's ranges, May–June, 1915" (copy).
[46] *Ibid.*
[47] "Minute of Meeting of Directors," June 25, 1914; "Notice of Extraordinary General Meeting," November 25, 1918.

in the disposal of lands. Clay reported in 1915 that "land matters have been practically dead."[48]

The company's unceasing efforts to realize the most profit from the lands were paralleled by the struggle to cover operating expenses by sheep and cattle.[49] Sheep had not proved to be of appreciably greater value than cattle. As already mentioned, sheep were brought in because of the difficulty in ranging the cattle and because of the uncertainty of weather and climate. But sheep were not an unmixed blessing. Until wool prices jumped to meet the demand for uniforms during World War I, the expected dividend from wool was not realized. Sheep were perhaps even more susceptible to severe weather than cattle. Johnston reported heavy lamb losses in the spring of 1915, while the cattle remained in excellent condition.[50] The executive committee had announced earlier in the year that it planned to start building the cattle herd and reducing the sheep. Thus climate, and also altitude, restricted the number of sheep that could be run with profit.[51]

The war boosted sheep prices so rapidly that by the next spring Clay sought advice from the board on the possibility of selling all the sheep and paying off the preference shares if the sheep would bring $500,000. The board approved of

[48] "Thirty-second Annual General Meeting," March 25, 1915.
[49] Letter from A. Thomson Clay, Sec., to John Clay, Jr., May 28, 1914, James T. Craig Collection, Western History Research Center, Laramie, Wyoming.
[50] "Report by Mr. J. C. Johnston to Directors. . . ." Also see, "Copy of Manager's report for month ending December 31, 1915," James T. Craig Collection. This sixteen-page report gives a clear and concise account of the detail and the scope of a manager's job and of the problems of running a company the size of the Swan Company.
[51] "Thirty-second Annual General Meeting," March 25, 1915.

the sale if such a possibility occurred.[52] However, one member of the board, Alexander McNab, returning after a long illness, dissented on the grounds that the sale of the sheep would leave the company without funds to meet expenses and taxes and would force a premature sale of the property.[53] James T. Craig, one of the three members of the executive committee, agreed with him. If there was any prospect of selling the land, then the scheme of selling the sheep to clear off the preference shares was good. Otherwise they would have to sell some land each year to keep going. The 60,000 sheep at $8 a head, and 4,000 cattle at $70 a head, would net $760,000—enough to meet the preference shares and leave some for the future. However, at wartime prices the returns from wool, lambs, calves, and fat cows, as well as steers, bucks, and the classes usually sold, would in two years' time clear off the preference shares. The number of sheep would have to be reduced at any rate, since "all of Goshen Hole" was gone.[54]

The executive committee, after careful consideration, came to the conclusion "that till we see a natural steady demand arise for our lands we cannot well turn off our sheep and be in rather a precarious position for income."[55] What the company did was sell all the sheep and cattle they possibly could, yet retained enough to keep their land occupied and, they hoped, to provide income to meet ordinary expenses. In 1916, 44,820 head of sheep were sold

[52] "Minute of Meeting of Directors," January 20, 1916.
[53] "Minute of Meeting," February 17, 1916.
[54] "Statement for the Directors of the Swan Land & Cattle Co., from James T. Craig, at Meeting of Directors," Minute of Meeting of Directors, April 20, 1916.
[55] *Ibid.*

for $220,800; 614 cattle for $22,220, and all stock horses for $4,000. The receipts from these sales, plus a wool clip of $137,000, netted the company $383,200 that year.[56]

Both sheep and cattle provided an excellent return during the war. The board could report to the shareholders at their meeting in March, 1917, that the debit balance had been extinguished. Chairman Johnston, who had spent considerable time on the ranges the past year, was able to lay the fortunes and future of the company before the shareholders.[57]

By 1917, the lands amounted to 268,000 acres in the plains division and an ever-decreasing amount of "free lands" in the eastern division. Of the 40,000 acres the company originally controlled in eastern Wyoming, only a very limited amount remained. The restricted use of the range and the high prices of the war had reduced the sheep herd from 101,898 in 1913 to 47,971 in 1916. Cattle had been reduced for the same reasons. However, Johnston believed that the company must continue to run livestock to pay for the operation of the range. Since most of the income from the sale of sheep and cattle had been derived from a capital asset, such income could not be used to pay dividends. Except for the fact that the company now had money invested in other enterprises and working for them—some forty thousand pounds in American Treasury bills and Liberty bonds—they had issued only small dividends throughout the war.[58]

The first decade and a half of the twentieth century saw remarkable changes in the operation of the ranch and the

[56] "Meeting of Executive Committee," Chugwater, Wyoming, November 15, 1916.
[57] "Thirty-fourth Annual General Meeting," April 30, 1917.
[58] *Ibid.*

beginning of financial stability. Along with the changes in operation came changes almost as remarkable in the management of the company. Following the dismissal of Clay as manager in 1896, Al Bowie assumed the position of manager in America; William Dawson succeeded Bowie in 1907. In Scotland the board also underwent some significant changes. In 1896, James Shepherd succeeded Colin J. Mackenzie as chairman of the board. Alexander McNab became chairman in 1906, and Thomas Murray served as secretary from the death of Finlay Dun in 1897, until 1913. In 1913, George Prentice became chairman, and A. Thomson Clay, secretary.

The most significant change in management came in 1912, when John Clay became a member of the Edinburgh board and the American executive committee was formed. Clay served as chairman of the committee, and associated with him were James T. Craig, the former manager of Western Ranches, one of the outstanding stockmen in Wyoming, and M. R. Johnson, the manager.[59] Management of the ranges under Bowie, Dawson, and Johnson had proved unsatisfactory, and it was hoped that the committee could provide better management.[60]

In 1913 the Swan Land and Cattle Company and the Colorado and Southern Railway became instrumental in the organization of the new townsite for Chugwater. Net acreage in the town site was nearly 400 acres. The Swan Company had five tracts of land amounting to 76.19 acres. M. R. Johnson, who had experience in town sites, was

[59] "Thirtieth Annual Report," March 19, 1913. Frank M. Johnson, the company's engineer, was the manager's son.

[60] See Clay, *My Life on the Range*, 205–206, and the annual reports for the years covered. Clay had been responsible for the appointment of M. R. Johnson, who was considered an expert in land matters.

placed in charge of the sale and the purchase thereof.[61] They proved to be something of a disappointment, however. It was believed that they would sell for $12,000 to $15,000, but they brought only about half that amount.[62] The greatest concern of the company in regard to the town sites was that of water, which the Swan Company drew from the Colorado and Southern Railway well.[63] Like the rest of the land, the town sites did not realize the immediate return anticipated. (The remainder of the lands were sold in 1950 to a Chugwater area farmer.)

In 1915, George Prentice, chairman of the board, died. He was succeeded the following year by James C. Johnston, a man more familiar with the ranch and livestock industry in America than had been any previous chairman or any member of the board, with the possible exception of John Clay. In the same year, 1916, M. R. Johnson tendered his resignation as manager, and Curtis Templin was appointed in his stead.[64]

Clay had notified the board in January that he was stepping down from the leadership of the American executive committee, where he had served since its inception in 1912, and that James T. Craig would assume responsibility for range management. Curtis Templin was appointed first to look after the store, bank, and office work and then to act as manager. Templin was thirty-one years old at the time and a native of Nebraska. He had worked for Clay

[61] "Minutes of Board Meeting," February 12, 1914.

[62] "Minutes of Meeting of Directors," June 26, 1914.

[63] A. Thomson Clay to John Clay, May 28, 1914, James T. Craig Collection.

[64] "Minutes of Committee of Directors," June 17, 1915; "Meeting of Directors," June 1, 1915; "Thirty-third Annual Report," March 31, 1916; and "Thirty-fourth Annual Report," April 30, 1917.

for about ten years, first at John Clay and Company in Chicago in 1905 and then at the Stock Growers National Bank in Cheyenne.[65]

Templin was an energetic young man and under the able tutelage of James T. Craig worked wonders on the range in a short time. According to Johnston, a "regular transformation" occurred after Templin took over. "Drunkenness, sloth, incompetence, disloyalty and even in some cases dishonesty have been succeeded by sobriety, energy, resourcefulness, loyalty and honesty." Jealousy and antagonism disappeared, and for the first time there was cooperation on the range.[66]

The manager's report for December, 1916, not only demonstrates Templin's ability as manager but also illustrates the detailed and complex operation of the Swan Company. Templin reported:

> The sheep of the Western Division which were placed on Sybille for the winter, consisting originally of 6226 ewes, have been split up on account of breeding season which commenced on November 20th. Mr. Morris reports that all bucks will be taken from the herds on January 2nd and placed at the Morris ranch where they will be fed corn and given special attention for the balance of the winter. We believe he is running the best of the ewes in two bands in the country adjacent to and along Sybille. He has cut out 214 culls which he is feeding at the Morris ranch 4 oz. of corn and all the hay they can eat. These he reports in very poor condition, a number of which may not winter. He has

---

[65] "Minute of Meeting of Directors of Swan Land and Cattle Company, Limited," January 7, 1915.

[66] "Report by Mr. J. C. Johnston to Directors of the Swan Land and Cattle Company, Ltd., upon his visit to the Company's ranges, May–June, 1915" (copy).

also at the Morris ranch a second cut of 1400 head of ewes which are thin and run mostly to old sheep, which he is herding in the country adjacent and brings in at night and gives them all the hay they will eat, and each morning two sacks of corn, or perhaps 180 lbs. These sheep are not in first-class condition and will need special attention. It seems that it was an error to not mouth out these sheep a little closer in the fall and dispose of at least a car or two more. . . . Of the 3125 ewe lambs which are being fed at the Two Bar ranch Mr. Morris reports only a loss of 6 head to date. They are doing nicely and are on a daily feed of 2 oz. of corn and 1 oz. of oats with what alfalfa they will eat. The hay, however, is of very poor quality, and anything but first-class lamb feed. He believes however, the lambs are doing very satisfactorily.

Templin demonstrated a real awareness of numbers of animals, locations, and conditions. This knowledge enabled him and the committee to seek the most efficient use of the company's property and personnel.

The weather received due attention. The following brief excerpt attests to the effect of weather on the total ranch operation:

The last 15 days of the month we had considerable blustery and cold weather. In fact there has been almost real winter weather here. On the Plains the thermometer has registered during that time as low as 27 degrees below whereas along the Chugwater district and in Goshen Hole we believe it has not been colder than 12 degrees below.

Although no suggestion is offered about what conditions were necessary to constitute "real winter weather," every sack of grain, bale of hay, and meadow was accounted for and evaluated in regard to the coming winter.

The cattle were so placed on the many ranches that each class could be best cared for during the coming winter months. Those at the Neilson Ranch had

> been receiving all the hay they would eat, for the last three weeks, 73 cows with perhaps as many suckling calves. These are late calves, some of them very young, practically none of which have been branded. Many of these cows are very old and in very poor condition and will need special attention in order to keep them up until spring. We are giving them a ration of cotton seed cake with the idea of keeping them in as good shape as possible so that they will give some milk for the calves which are too young to wean.

Several of the ranch houses, the Bard in particular, had been rebuilt, added to, or placed in operational condition. Bunk houses, stables, barns, corrals, and fences on many ranches had also received necessary attention. Irrigation ditches, headgates, and laterals, many of which had been destroyed during summer storms, had been replaced or repaired, although several still needed attention. The Morris Ranch had been leased for five years, and the Morrises had been retained to operate the Two Bar Ranch—Morris as foreman of the cattle operation and Mrs. Morris to provide meals and quarters for hired hands and visitors who showed up at the ranch.

Losses had also occurred among the cattle and sheep. On the plains about ten thousand lambs had been lost as a result of bad weather. Many calves had also been lost when they were trailed across the plains:

> The weather was especially bad, May weather being worse than April, and as many of the calves were very young they were unable to stand the hard snowy weather and hard cold

storms which prevailed at that time. We also suffered a loss of calves for the reason that after one of the snow storms the sun came out especially hot and sunburned the teats of the cows and they became swollen and sore and in many cases refused to let the calves suckle. Many of the calves for this reason were either bummed so that they were of little value, or even died. . . . We also lost at that time several yearlings which unfortunately had just been castrated before they were started on the trip across.

Other expenses included the purchase of eight manure spreaders ($1,000) and the employment of two large and one small manure-spreading gangs which the manager calculated cost $30 a day to operate. New haying equipment had to be purchased for some ranches. Some legal expenses were involved in establishing section lines. A wool rick at the M Bar Ranch was swept away in the spring flood, at a loss of $3,500 worth of wool.

Although the report of December, 1916, was not an official year-end report, it did cover a variety of activities, expenses, and operations during the preceding year. The year's operation had been expensive—more than anticipated—but the manager was able to report a balance of twenty-five thousand dollars in the First National Bank of Chicago and about seven thousand dollars in the Chugwater Valley Bank.[67] It is little wonder that the next spring John Clay informed the directors: "Mr. Templin's extraordinary activity and excellent judgement is gradually building the affairs of the company into good shape."[68]

By the spring of 1917 the Swan Land and Cattle Com-

[67] "Copy of the Manager's Report for the Month Ending, December 31, 1915," James T. Craig Collection.
[68] "Minute of Meeting of Directors . . . ," February 17, 1916.

pany was, in all probability, in as good condition as it ever had been or would be. It had a landed property of nearly three hundred thousand acres, fifty thousand sheep, a few thousand cattle, and about forty thousand pounds invested in Liberty bonds and Treasury notes. Wartime prices had greatly boosted the value of its livestock and land. Its one great difficulty was the arrangement of its capital investment in Scotland. Capital could not be used to pay dividends on the preference shares, and dividends could not be paid on the ordinary shares until the preference shares were dealt with. The time and money were at hand for a better scheme of capitalization.

CHAPTER VII

The New Swan Company

By 1917 the high prices received from sheep, wool, and cattle during the war, plus the sale of some very choice lands, had accumulated a credit in the company's account. Both classes of shareholders were eager to receive some return on their investment, but the arrangement of the share capital made it difficult to satisfy one class without harm to the other.

The situation was explained in a letter to the shareholders before the annual meeting.[1] The company's share capital consisted of ten thousand preference shares of ten pounds each, fully paid, entitled to a 5 per cent annual dividend, and seventy-five thousand ordinary shares of two pounds each, fully paid. No preference dividend had been declared since 1911. The preference shareholders were entitled to dividends only out of profits earned in trade by the com-

---

[1] "To the Shareholders of the Swan Land and Cattle Company, Limited, April 20, 1917" (letter), "Proceedings in Scheme of Arrangement with Preference Shareholders, 1917–1918 (bound book); hereafter cited as "Proceedings, 1917–18." Unless otherwise indicated, all information in this chapter is taken from the Swan files of the WRCIS.

pany. No preference dividends could be paid out of capital assets. Preference dividends from 1912 to 1916 would have amounted to twenty-five thousand pounds, and, although the company had forty thousand pounds on hand, it was necessary to retain most of this money to replenish the sheep sold during the high price period of the war; therefore, there was no chance of paying off the preference capital in the immediate future.[2]

But a portion of the forty thousand pounds was available for paying off part of the preference shares, and the board proposed a new scheme at its annual meeting. Since the shares were receiving no dividend, they were a drug on the market. The preference shareholders could not receive dividends, nor could they use the capital already expended for any other investment. The ordinary shareholders could not hope to realize any substantial returns until the land was sold. The board proposed, therefore, that the "Preference Shareholders should cancel all arrears, while Ordinary Shareholders should waive any claim to Dividend till the prior debt is repaid." A portion of the preference capital could be redeemed by capital already on hand and the balance by debentures, "the next best thing to cash."[3]

The board proposed the cancellation of the preference shares by repayment of part in cash and the balance in debenture stock created for that purpose. The outline of this scheme was approved at an extraordinary general meeting immediately following the annual meeting in 1917.[4] The preference shareholder was thus exchanging non–dividend-paying shares—which were nearly impossible to

---

[2] *Ibid.*
[3] "Thirty-fourth Annual General Meeting," April 30, 1917.
[4] *Ibid.*

sell—for debentures with a guaranteed annual income which could be redeemed by capital from the sale of land. The scheme was of even greater importance to the ordinary shareholder. Company overhead would be reduced from five thousand to three thousand pounds a year—the difference between 5 per cent on one hundred thousand pounds of preference shares, and 6 per cent on fifty thousand pounds of debentures. There was also the probability that within a very few years all the debentures would be redeemed and the ordinary shareholders would be "masters of their own house."

The court was petitioned in June, 1917, for permission to rearrange the capital of the company. The canceled shares were paid off, one-half in cash with 6 per cent a year from December 31, 1916, and one-half in debenture stock of 6 per cent a year. The borrowing power of the company was limited to one hundred thousand pounds. The ordinary shareholder could receive no dividend until the entire debenture stock and interest had been redeemed. Under this scheme the capital of the company was reduced to £150,-000, consisting of 75,000, fully-paid £2 shares, with an additional £100,000 in debenture stock.[5] Separate meetings for approval were held by both ordinary and preference shareholders. Both approved of the reduction scheme.[6] The debenture stockholders were notified on February 26, 1920, that the company was prepared to pay the debenture stock on March 31, 1920.[7]

[5] "Petition of the Swan Land and Cattle Company, Limited, to the Lords of Council and Session Second Division," June 25, 1917, "Proceedings, 1917–18."
[6] "Notice of Meetings," July 26, 1917, and "Extraordinary General Meeting," August 9, 1917, "Proceedings, 1917–18."
[7] Letter to Debenture Stockholders, February 26, 1920.

In brief, in 1917 the company, finding itself in a financial situation in which neither class of stockholder could benefit, proposed a reorganization of its capital stock. So successful was the proposal that while the scheme was still in court the preference shares rose from £6, 16s.3d for a £10 share to £9, 5s., and ordinary shares, from 22s. to 29s.6d. Both of these shares, unmarketable for years, now became active.[8] With the new scheme the company reduced its debt by £50,000 and within two years had redeemed even that amount. By 1920 the company's capital was represented by £150,000 in 75,000 £2 shares, and it was still making a profit.

Although prices failed in 1920, the company continued to realize gradual return from its land and other assets. In 1923 the board found itself in a position to make a repayment on the company's capital. The proposed repayment was a moderate one of four shillings a share, but the board believed that as the company gradually realized on its lands it would from time to time make other repayments.[9]

According to the companies acts each repayment of capital required a special resolution, passed and confirmed at separate meetings, a court confirmation order in which permission must be obtained from all creditors for capital reduction or repayment, and a registration of the confirmation order. Gaining permission from all creditors was tedious and time consuming, and so the board proposed that a major reduction in ordinary-share capital be made and replaced by a debenture loan.[10]

[8] "Extraordinary General Meeting," August 9, 1917, "Proceedings, 1917–18."

[9] Letter to Shareholders, September 11, 1923, "Proceedings for Carrying out Scheme of Arrangement with Shareholders 1923–1924"; hereafter cited as "Proceedings, 1923–24."

[10] *Ibid.*

The 1923–24 scheme of arrangement again reduced the capital of the company, this time from £150,000 in 75,000 £2 shares to £7,500 in 75,000 2s. shares. In place of the canceled shares the shareholders were to receive 38s. for each share in debenture stock to the total amount of £142,500. Such debentures would receive no interest, and no bonus or dividend could be paid on the shares until the total debenture stock was redeemed. The company allowed twenty years for the redemption of the debentures, and no redeemed debenture could be reissued.[11] The borrowing powers of the company were increased to £200,000.

The chairman, James C. Johnston, had explained the purpose of the non–interest-bearing debenture to the shareholders at a previous meeting. Whatever money was received was to be divided immediately among the shareholders. If interest were paid on the debentures, a sum would have to be set aside each year to provide for the interest. The business was not one in which there was a "steady yearly revenue," and so there was always danger of being forced to sell land at an inopportune moment to meet the interest.[12] At the confirmation meeting of the shareholders, the directors announced that they would be able to distribute a dividend of five shillings a share as soon as the scheme was approved by the court, which action took place on March 1, 1924. By October the directors were able to redeem an additional 10 per cent of the 1924 debenture stock.[13]

[11] Notice of Meeting to be held on November 29, 1923, "Proceedings, 1923–24."

[12] "Extraordinary Meeting of the Shareholders of the Company," September 21, 1923. At the extraordinary general meeting held on November 29, 1923, the shareholders were further encouraged in the promotion of the scheme by a promise of return on the capital.

The years 1917–25 were the most profitable years for the original company's shareholders and investors. If dividends were not great, at least there was an immediate return of the capital invested, which could be more profitably invested. This, of course, was the expressed intent of the 1917–18 reorganization scheme. With the redemption of the 1917 debentures the capital investment of the company consisted of the ordinary shares which could not be paid off without a great amount of legal detail. For this reason the 1923–24 reorganization scheme reduced the ordinary shares to two shillings each and placed most of the capital in debentures which could be easily retired.

The progress of the company during these years was even more remarkable when the problems with which it was confronted are considered. In 1917 the 640 Acre Homestead Act was passed, and settlers began moving onto the government sections of the plains. Settlers would be forced out if a few dry years occurred, but in the meantime they greatly interfered with grazing. The problem in 1919 was no longer finding enough winter feed but finding enough summer grazing. The company could handle 65,000 head of sheep in the winter but found it increasingly difficult to graze that many.[14] Settlers were such an interference that between 1913 and 1920 the American executive committee found it necessary to purchase from the state of Wyoming 6,806 acres under some twenty-two different contracts at

---

[13] "Interlocutor in Petition of the Swan Land & Cattle Company, Limited . . . for Sanction to Scheme of Arrangement . . . . (copy), "Proceedings, 1923–24"; and Letter to Holders of the 1924 Debenture Stock of the Company, October 17, 1924.

[14] "Report of Proceedings of the Extraordinary General Meeting of the Company," December 4, 1919.

a total cost of $79,058.10, just to ensure adequate grazing land.[15]

At its annual meeting in 1921 the board announced the end of the years of prosperity: "At the Shareholders Meeting of May 20th, 1920, it was indicated that the high prices of the four preceding war years were not likely to be maintained, but no one anticipated that the fall would be so unprecedentedly complete, rapid, and drastic."[16] Second-grade wool was unsaleable, and no offer could be obtained for the 1920 clip, although that of 1919 had sold at fifty-five cents on the sheep's back. The price of sheep had fallen from fifteen and eighteen dollars to five and eight dollars. The depression in agriculture forced the dry farmer to give up his land. Since most of it had been government sections, its settlement had ruined the use of the range for the company. While the depression gave the company an excellent opportunity to regain control of its grazing by purchase of the homestead lands, it also rendered the sale of its own lands next to impossible.[17] Clay, in a letter to the board, stated that there was some improvement in the market and operating expenses had been reduced by nearly half—primarily by a reduction in salaries—but that land was impossible to sell.[18]

Burdened though it was by the postwar depression and by its ungainly financial structure, the company realized enough return to reduce its capital to almost nothing. In the forty-one years since its founding, the share capital of the company had shrunk from nine hundred thousand

---

[15] Curtis Templin, "List of Certificate of Purchase Covering Lands Purchased from the State of Wyoming under contract, December 5, 1924."
[16] "Thirty-eighth Annual General Meeting," April 8, 1921.
[17] *Ibid.*
[18] "Thirty-ninth Annual General Meeting," April 3, 1922.

pounds in 1886 to seventy-five hundred pounds in 1924. However, it must be remembered that of this amount six hundred thousand pounds had been lost rather than redeemed or repaid.

In spite of the great energy and resourcefulness of the company, there was one omnipresent problem: taxes. British and American income taxes, both corporate and individual, were devouring the profits of the company. To relieve itself of this great burden, the organization had three alternatives; liquidate, transfer, or sell. While every shareholder hoped for liquidation, that solution was unacceptable on at least two counts: the income tax would still have to be paid on all money remitted to Britain, and liquidation meant a forced sale of the land, which would be disastrous with the depressed land value at the time. Transferring the management of the company to the United States would relieve the company of the tax burden but would place the management outside the control of any shareholder or director not in America. Sale of the company's property was perhaps the more desirable of the alternatives, but to make such a sale involved time, and meanwhile taxes must be paid. By 1924 the depression of the early twenties and the double income tax had forced the company to seek a new scheme of organization and a new location.

John Clay probably made the preliminary proposition for a change in the residence of the company.[19] According to the tax acts, residence could be determined neither by the place of registration of the company nor by the place

[19] "Minute of Meeting of Directors, March 12, 1924," *Minute Book No. 6*. "The Secretary was instructed to write Mr. Clay that the Directors were greatly interested in the subject matter of his letter; that they saw great possibilities of the scheme."

where the business was actually located but rather by the location of its control and responsibility.[20] As long as the board in Edinburgh remained in control of management, it would be considered a resident company for the purposes of taxation. Within less than two weeks the company's attorneys had outlined the major points of a scheme to form an American company and issue the stock of that organization for the shares of the present one. In brief, the British shareholder would become a creditor of a foreign company. As such there was no liability for income tax on payments received for the satisfaction of a capital debt.[21]

Before the end of the year members of the board met to discuss some way of avoiding the income taxes for the next fiscal year, which would begin April 5, 1925.[22] However, it soon became clear that an American company could not be formed in time to avoid it. Even transference of the management to America in the short time remaining was doubtful. A rush program by the directors, however, managed to devise the necessary amendments to the Articles of Association and inform the shareholders of the urgency of a meeting to act by the end of February. A letter to the shareholders not only explained the established practice of amending the Articles of Association for the purpose of transferring the business to American control but also outlined the broader scheme of selling to an American com-

[20] Fraser to Gibson, May 26, 1925.
[21] Ballingall to Fraser, June 6, 1924; "Preliminary and Provisional Estimate (made up by Winston, Strawn and Shaw's letter to John Clay & Co., July 15, 1925) of Expense of Incorporating American Company."
[22] Gibson to Fraser, November 7, 1924; "Supplementary Memorial for the Swan Land & Cattle Company, Limited, for Opinion and Advice of Council, November 21, 1924."

pany.[23] At a meeting, early in March, 1925, the chairman informed the shareholders:

> Your Directors have been anxiously considering whether it might not, in some way, be possible to relieve you from the pressure of the millstone of double taxation as regards profits. First let me say that we do not grudge the payment of American income tax—at present 2s.6d. in the pound—because our profits are made in the United States, but when, on the top of this 4s.6d. per pound, in all practically 7s. per pound, or about 35 per cent of the profits, the burden becomes intolerable, and for some time past your Directors have been searching for a practicable and legal method of dealing with this problem. I understand that the British Government have been approached to deal with it by granting the same relief as is granted by them to companies trading in the Colonies, but that they have declined to do so. Your Directors therefore had to explore some other method by which this crushing burden could be reduced. Remember practically none of your profits are earned in this country.[24]

That meeting transferred "all of the Company's business and affairs whatsoever in the Territory or State of Wyoming or elsewhere in the United States of America" to an American board to the exclusion of any other board of directors.[25]

By March 9, 1925, the complete affairs of the company were in the hands of three men, John Clay, James T. Craig, and Curtis Templin. Throughout the remainder of the year

[23] Letter to Shareholders, February 26, 1925.
[24] "Extraordinary General Meeting of Company," March 9, 1925; "Notices of Meetings Annual-Special 1925–1926" (folder).
[25] *Ibid.*

the Edinburgh board continued its efforts to transfer the entire undertaking to an organization incorporated in the United States.[26]

In the late summer there was one brief bubble of hope for disposal of the property by other means. On August 20 the secretary of the company received the following telegram from John Clay:

> Present conditions indicate can sell this fall and next spring wool and other liquid assets net seven fifty thousand dollars This would pay off debentures leaving balance for future disposal Land matters uncertain but think we can lease plains enough pay carrying charges Chug Sybille and other lands somewhat uncertain Probably no heavy loss as there is some inquiry for land We could operate or lease as thought best You consider British taxes We consider our taxes Advise promptly at least before twenty ninth.[27]

This message was succeeded a few days later by the gloomy:

> Committee been in conference two days with aid of Connor Have reached conclusion impossible carry lands without sheep No demand lands either leasing or sale Would have to operate property and cannot find better way than at present Will sell ten thousand oldest sheep Hope send you hundred fifty thousand dollars end year.[28]

By early November the two law firms Winston, Strawn, and Shaw in Chicago and Fraser, Stodart, and Ballingall in Edinburgh were carrying on extensive correspondence

---

[26] *Forty-second Annual General Meeting*, April 23, 1925.

[27] Gibson to Clay, August 28, 1925. A copy of the telegram was included in the letter.

[28] Gibson to Clay, August 31, 1925. Clay was further advised to hold the $150,000 until the new company was organized.

in regard to an American company. Both firms knew what they wanted, but each was somewhat ignorant of the laws of the other's country. The proper sequence for liquidation, sale, and issuance of new stock had to be worked out to save the most in time, expenses, and assets involved. Ultimately it was decided that the best order of activity would be to liquidate the Scottish company and then sell or transfer the assets to the American company. Only a matter of three or four weeks could be allowed for such a transfer. Incorporation in Delaware was apparently chosen for that reason.[29]

In January, 1926, the board petitioned the court for the necessary legal action on liquidation and transfer. The petition placed December 31, 1925, as the legal date of sale of the Scottish company to a corporation to be incorporated under the laws of Delaware. Share capital or total authorized stock of the Delaware corporation was placed at $750,000 in 75,000 shares of $10 each. There was in addition an authorized loan capital of $1,144,585 divided into $544,585 in first bearer bonds, upon which no interest could be paid until December 31, 1943, and $600,000 in second bearer bonds, which could draw no interest until December 31, 1948. The total assets transferred were $1,894,585.[30]

To the shareholders of the Scottish company, the capital of the new company represented an exchange of 2s. shares for $10 shares. The rate of exchange as set by the company was $5 for each £1. The £7,500 in ordinary-share capital was now increased to £150,000. Thus the 95 per cent reduc-

<hr>

[29] Fraser, Stodart and Ballingall to Winston, Strawn and Shaw, December 18, 1925.

[30] "Petition of the Swan Land and Cattle Company, Limited, to Lords of Council and Session, Second Division," January 19, 1926.

tion made in the share capital by the 1924 scheme was regained.

Curtis Templin, manager of the company at Chugwater, made a belated effort to have the company incorporated in Wyoming and to change the name. Early in January, Templin laid his case before the attorneys at Chicago either to retain the name Swan Land and Cattle Company or to change it to the Swan Company, instead of the proposed Swan Land and Sheep Company. The company dealt primarily in land, and its future in sheep was limited, but it was universally referred to as the Swan Company, and this short and convenient name would allow it to engage in any business of its choice.[31] Templin was successful, and the new organization officially became the Swan Company.

In the second matter Templin was not so successful. The company's Cheyenne attorney, Avery Haggard, after examining the certificates for the new company, stated the desirability of forming a domestic corporation. According to the laws of Wyoming a Delaware-incorporated company was legally as "foreign" as a Scottish company. Incorporation was more expensive in Delaware than in Wyoming, but more important were the favors, both official and unofficial, which the company could enjoy if it was incorporated in Wyoming. To incorporate in Wyoming would cost $245. A foreign corporation must pay a fee of $10 and an additional $1 for each $1,000 value, or, in the case of the Delaware company, $1,010. The most obvious and important advantage, however, was the treatment an organization could expect at the hands of the state:

It is common experience that public officials, such as tax

[31] Templin to Winston, Strawn and Shaw, January 2, 1926.

assessors and County Commissioners, show a more generally friendly spirit towards domestic corporations than towards
foreign ones. . . . Moreover the company is an extensive
holder of leases of state lands. In the leasing of state lands
the statutes provide that in many instances preference shall
be given to an applicant who is a resident of the State, and
the state boards oftener show a deposition to favor resident
as against foreign corporation.[32]

A few days later Templin pleaded the same case with John
Clay. Apparently so much of the legal action and printing
had already been based on the assumption that the company would be incorporated in Delaware that it was too
late to change.[33]

In February, 1926, the final details of the transaction
were arranged. Incorporation for a new company began in
Delaware on February 11, 1926, and the Swan Company
was organized in that state on February 15, 1926.[34] The
Swan Company of Delaware entered into a trust agreement
with the First Trust and Savings Bank of Chicago, to issue
$544,585 in Series A deferred bonds, which replaced the
remainder of the 1924 debenture issue and $600,000 Series
B deferred bonds. Approval by the shareholders of the
details of the scheme of transfer were made on March 12,
1926.[35]

[32] Haggard to Templin, January 3, 1926.
[33] Templin to Clay, January 27, 1926. See also Gibson to Fraser,
Stodart and Ballingall, February 10, 1926.
[34] Cables from Winston, Strawn and Shaw to Fraser, Stodart and
Ballingall, February 11, February 16, 1926.
[35] "Agreement Between the Swan Company of Delaware and the First
Trust and Savings Bank of Chicago, Illinois." Included are copies of the
bill of sale, the deed, an agreement on the part of the new company to
assume the liabilities of the old, and "Notice of Extraordinary General
Meeting to be Held March 12, 1926."

While approval was acquired, faith in the new venture was not unanimous. At least one shareholder had doubts:

I have the impression that all the shares of the Coy. (including mine) were converted into debentures in order to facilitate the reduction of capital and these, I suppose, represent the 1924 Debenture Stock referred to in the Scheme. But as it appears that this Stock is to be exchanged for First Bonds that carry no interest for the next 18 years it looks as though it would be equally profitable to some of the present holders (myself included) to put the stock in the fire.[36]

The secretary, however, may have cooled the fire when he replied that the 131 shares of 2s. each which the shareholder had were last quoted on the market at 8s., and his £190 of 1924-debenture stock, which would carry no interest until 1943, was selling only at 56 per cent of its face value.[37] The last report submitted by the Swan Land and Cattle Company, Ltd., was at its forty-third annual meeting held on March 30, 1926, and concluded the business of the company as of December 31, 1925. That report listed total assets of $1,042,831.23. Less than one-half ($492,784) represented land and improvements, approximately one-fourth represented livestock, and the remainder represented investments and savings.[38] The first report of the Swan Company listed its assets at $1,808,459.61, with land and improvements accounting for over one-half ($1,096,823.48). However, livestock—including the wool clip—accounted for nearly one-third of the

[36] Shareholder (J. M. Powers) to Gibson, January 20, 1926.
[37] Gibson to Powers, February 1, 1926.
[38] "Forty-third Annual Report," March 30, 1926.

total, or $655,750, with the remainder in investments and savings.[39] The directors increased the value of the land and livestock by some 90 per cent to keep pace with its increase in capitalization.

Throughout the depression decade the Swan Company did little except hang on. That in itself was remarkable, but it was also a testimony to the expert management of Curtis Templin. More land was purchased than disposed of, the purchases being made to consolidate range lands rather than increase the holdings. The company conserved its energy and capital, consolidated its holdings, and made its operating expenses from sheep and cattle. They were lean years but not disastrous ones.

It was not until the war years that Templin managed to begin the liquidation of the company. In 1943 the company made its first large sale of land. Two large blocks of land totaling 106,720 acres were sold for an average price of $2.21 an acre. That same year the Series A bonds were repaid in full.[40] The following year 60,187 acres on the Laramie Plains were sold for $2.22 an acre, while the Mule-shoe, T. H., Jones, Whitcomb, and Bard ranches in the eastern division, amounting collectively to 13,288 acres, were sold at an average of $17.05 an acre. A repayment of 40 per cent was made on the Series B bonds, and arrangements were made for the remaining 60 per cent to be paid on April 2, 1945.[41]

Throughout the remainder of the forties the balance of the land was sold. The Carlin, Neilson, and CMD ranches,

---

[39] "The Swan Company, First Annual Report and Balance Sheet," February 11, 1927.
[40] "Eighteenth Annual Report and Balance Sheet," February 14, 1944.
[41] "Nineteenth Annual Report and Balance Sheet," February 19, 1945.

plus some small plots in Platte County and near Goshen Hole—a total of 42,830 acres—were sold for $147,882 net, at an average of $3.45 an acre. The Two-Bar and Shearing Pens ranches—97,775 acres—were sold in 1946, for $316,670 net, at an average of $3.24 an acre. In 1947 four Chugwater ranches, the LD, M-Bar, TY, and Kelly ranches—24,580 acres—were sold for $320,877 at an average of $13.05 an acre.

The same year the Naffziger Ranch, the remaining Laramie Plains grazing lands of 20,293 acres in Albany County, and a number of small scattered plots of land were sold. The total land sales for 1947 were 51,873 acres, for a net $416,168, at an average of $8.02 an acre. With the sale of 1,450 acres of land in 1948, the board announced that "all lands have now been sold with the exception of the Home Ranch at Chugwater consisting of 2,183.24 acres." At a special meeting of the stockholders on November 27, 1950, this ranch, valued at $36,327.35, was given to Curtis Templin, in reward for his dedicated services as manager of the ranch for the past thirty-five years. Templin has increased the ranch to some 4,400 acres today. The entire herd of sheep—about 22,000 head—were sold in 1947 at an average price of $12.81 a head. A substantial increase in sheep had developed over the past four years with an annual increase in value of about $2.00 a head. All livestock were disposed of in 1950.

The final repayment of $360,000 had been made on the Series B bonds on April 2, 1945, and the stockholders at their annual meeting in 1950 approved of the complete liquidation and dissolution of the company and announced a dividend of $12.00 a share. A final dividend of $1.55 a share was paid on December 20, 1951, and the company was dissolved.[42]

The Swan had begun in a burst of ambition, speculation, and western glamour that ended with the great "die up" of 1886–87. The early decades of the twentieth century, up to the outbreak of World War I, were times of great trial for the company, but it survived and retained its holdings. War prices brought real prosperity to the company for the first time since 1886, and for the duration of the war and the years immediately following, the company enjoyed a degree of prosperity. The hallmark of the company from that time on was "business." There were deputations to the ranges and visits by shareholders, but these reports speak only of sheep, cattle, disposal of land, taxes, costs, improvements, and hope. There are no descriptions of roundups, hardships, good food, and bad whisky to indicate that the West of Alec Swan and Colin Mackenzie was still alive. Not even a Finlay Dun with a paint brush appeared to break the monotony.

[42] These figures are taken from the annual reports and balance sheets of the Swan Company covering the years 1945 through 1951, numbers 20th through 26th. These final reports are not included in the Swan Collection of the WRCIS, but were acquired from Curtis Templin by the author, as well as from an interview with Russell Staats, cashier of the Swan Company for the preceding forty-four years, on July 18, 1968, and an interview with Curtis Templin, manager of the company since 1915, on August 21, 1968.

CHAPTER VIII

Conclusion

WHEN Alexander Swan went to Scotland in 1882 to raise capital for a new company that would purchase the holdings of the three cattle companies of which he was president, he helped create one of the premier cattle companies of the era. The Swan Land and Cattle Company, Ltd., or as it was known locally, the Two Bar, was one of the largest and most durable of the major foreign companies. The company reportedly owned so many brands that it published its own brand book for the benefit of its foremen. For twenty years it ran thousands of cattle on a million acres of land in southeast Wyoming and for forty more years ran sheep and cattle on a slowly shrinking range. Of the great foreign companies only the Matador Land and Cattle Company and the Prairie Cattle Company rank with the Swan, and only the Matador enjoyed a longer and a more rewarding life than the Swan.

John Clay, associated with the company for most of his adult life, first as manager, replacing Alexander Swan, and then as a member of the American executive committee, stated in 1924 that in his thirty-five years of service with the company it had been "rather a hoodoo on the Horizon."[1]

Any adequate evaluation of the Swan Land and Cattle Company, as well as of the other great land and cattle companies, both foreign and domestic, must include its contribution to the development of the western cattle industry. A joint-stock company appeared to be the only successful means by which sufficient capital could be raised for the immediate development of the cattle industry in the West. Cattlemen's associations were adequate organizations for the control and stability of the industry, but they could not have produced the finance necessary for the rapid growth and expansion of the cattle business. The great contribution of the stockmen's association—in this particular case the Wyoming Stock Growers' Association—was its ability to obtain the most desirable legislation possible in behalf of the stock growers. The great contribution of the cattle company, such as the Swan Land and Cattle Company, was to make capital available for the development of the cattle industry. It would seem that the cattle company was a necessary forerunner to the cattlemen's association. A great many of the laws and practices adopted by the cattlemen were initiated by Alexander Swan or the Swan Company. In particular, selective breeding and seasonal rather than continual use of herd bulls were Swan innovations. On the other hand, the maverick law was passed over the opposition of Swan and other large cattle-company interests.

The financial returns of the Swan, similar to those of the other companies, varied according to the local, national, and international situations. During the first three years

[1] Clay, *My Life on the Range*, 222.

it returned a 25 per cent dividend.[2] From 1886 to 1892 the shareholders received no dividend, and the call on their shares rose from six pounds in 1883 to ten pounds, or fully paid, in 1892. In that year eight pounds of each ten-pound share was canceled. In short, the total loss for each shareholder for the period 1883–92 was about 55 per cent. No dividend was paid on the two-pound shares until 1897, and from that date to 1926, when the company was reorganized as an American company, a total of 65.625 per cent, or about 2 per cent a year, was realized.

When the American company was organized, the value of the shares was increased from £7,500 to £150,000—each 2s. share becoming a $10 share—and the unredeemed debentures were exchanged for bonds. Under the terms of the new company no dividend was paid to stockholders until both the Series A and Series B bonds were repaid. However from 1946 to 1951, when the final distribution was made, the shareholder received a 255.5 per cent return. This amounted to an annual dividend of 10 per cent.

The shareholder in the Scottish company received his money back in dividends but did not regain the 80 per cent loss of capital he had suffered in 1892. However, he still retained his shares, which were valued at two shillings and exchanged for ten-dollar shares, while the debentures he had received in 1924 were exchanged for bonds. In this manner he recovered approximately one-third of his loss of 1892. The cancellation of share capital as a result of the disasters of 1886–87 was typical of all the cattle companies. A large number of them never recovered from the loss. The Prairie wrote off capital and deducted cattle, and so did the Matador. Like Swan they continued to suffer from

[2] See Appendix D.

climatic conditions throughout much of the rest of the century.

The financial return of the company to the ordinary shareholder, who had been active from 1883 to 1950, was a modest one. It is, of course, illogical to assume that any shareholder survived those sixty-seven years, but if he had, his return would not have amounted to more than 2.5 per cent a year. Many more Americans became shareholders after 1926, and their investment was much more profitable. Since, however, the major holders of ordinary shares were also the holders of the debentures or preferred stock, the return was undoubtedly much greater than this accounting alone suggests. Nor was the profit derived from trading in stocks taken into consideration. Indeed, it is difficult to understand how an enterprise could have remained in existence over that number of years with no greater return than appears on the books.

It is equally difficult to discover why the Swan Company did not make a better showing. In 1883 it purchased at twenty-five dollars a head cattle which were according to certain authorities and to judge by the market price of the Swan cattle, well worth thirty to thirty-five dollars. Even if there were not as many cattle on the range as claimed, the company's cattle must still be considered an asset. It does appear obvious that the winter of 1886–87 was nearly disastrous. While the direct loss of cattle was heavy—15 to 20 per cent—an even greater loss resulted from the drastic drop in calves and the poor condition of cattle for market. The cancellation of capital in 1892 reflected these losses more than any other factor.

What does seem to stand out during the first twenty-five or thirty years of the company is poor management. The bickering at annual meetings, the establishment of a share-holders' committee to check on the board, the shuffling of officials, the activities of Finlay Dun all seem to point to poor leadership. John Clay regarded the early Swan board as somewhat inferior to that of other companies. Except for the first three years, when the ranch was left in the hands of Alexander Swan, not much growth ensued. The decision to stock the range with sheep in 1904 was not particularly successful. Sheep fared no better than, if as well as, cattle. The only reason the board offered for running sheep was that the range was no longer open and it was easier to take care of sheep than cattle. Other reasons may be suggested. It took four to five years for cattle to mature sufficiently for market and only a year for sheep. Sheep were marketable twice each year, once for wool, once for meat. But the wool market was more unpredictable than the dressed-meat trade, and mutton was never as popular as beef in the United States. It appears that the company missed a great opportunity in not capitalizing on what Swan had begun, namely, improved stock and selective breeding of cattle.

Under Swan's leadership improvement of the herds seemed to be the primary factor. Even before the founding of the Scottish company, Swan showed interest in improving the herds by using high-grade and purebred bulls, leaving the bulls with the herds only at the proper season to prevent too early calving and a loss of calves from bad weather. Dun's belief that the herds were too highly graded does not make much sense. The loss on the northern ranges in 1886–87 appeared to be much greater among Texas cattle than among high-grade cattle. That was clear in Dun's reports of the next summer. It is also contrary to what the small rancher was proving, as Tait's report indicated.

It was the quality of the herd, as well as the quantity, which apparently interested the Scots in the first place. During the tenure of Alexander Swan, and even thereafter, except for those years when climatic conditions forced the company to market poorly finished cattle, the Swan Company cattle brought top prices. In some years the price of Swan cattle was nearly twice that of Matador cattle. The fact that others realized the value of Alexander Swan in the cattle industry is witnessed by this comment from one who knew both, Swan and cattle. W. E. Guthrie commented in 1931:

> The Cattlemen of Wyoming even today owe a debt of gratitude to A. H. Swan which they little realize and can never repay, for his efforts in improving the breeding of range cattle. In the early days the Texas cow and the "scrub" bull were good enough. As early as 1877 Mr. Swan began buying for his range herd the best pure bred Hereford bulls he could find in Illinois and Iowa, and later imported a large number of England's best animals, both bulls and cows. To Mr. Swan more than to any other is due the introduction of pure bred Hereford bulls, the result of which may be seen now on almost every ranch in the state.[3]

Belated recognition came to Swan in 1960, when he was nominated to the Cowboy Hall of Fame in Oklahoma City. The *Wyoming State Tribune* announced Swan's nomination and reminded the present citizen of the state that "Swan developed near fabulous ranches, imported some of the first purebreds to Wyoming and the west, built stock-

[3] W. E. Guthrie, "Rise and Fall of the Open Range Cattle Business in Wyoming," *Omaha Daily Journal Stockman*, January 1, 1931.

yards, and was a leader in livestock organization and in civic development."[4] Swan was the fifth Wyoming resident to be nominated to the Cowboy Hall of Fame, sharing honors with former senators and governors—Francis E. Warren, Joseph M. Carey, and John B. Kendrick—and the Bear River valley pioneer trader, rancher, and cattleman John W. Myers.[5] Agnes Wright Spring, in her article nominating Swan for the Hall of Fame found him in good company elsewhere:

> In the Sirloin and Saddle Club, Chicago, hangs a portrait of Alexander Hamilton Swan, flanked on one side by Jesse Chisholm of the Chisholm Trail, and on the other by Sam Cowan, who for many years was traffic attorney of the American National Live Stock Association. On the wall across is Walter Farwell of the XIT Ranch, and on the other side is Heber Hord.[6]

To many in Wyoming, the Swan Company became a way of life—a hallmark for their state. One writer in the 1930's expressed it in this manner:

> Visitors coming into Platte County and making inquiries as to the ownership of the ranches along such streams as the Sybille, and the Chugwater are often amazed to learn that so large a percentage of these choice land holdings belong to the "Two Bar" or more properly speaking "the Swan Company." It seems that Fortune must have plucked out the heart of the country and tossed it into the lap of this body of favored sons.[7]

[4] *Wyoming State Tribune* (Cheyenne) March 9, 1960.
[5] *Ibid.*
[6] Agnes Wright Spring, "Alexander Hamilton Swan, Wyoming's Pioneer Cattle King" (MS), November 23, 1959, Alexander Swan 2d Collection, Western History Research Center, Laramie, Wyoming.
[7] Mildred E. Nelson, "The Old Two Bar," *Wheatland* (Wyoming) *Times*, August 10, 1933.

It may have been difficult for a visitor, especially one from the East who was used to the idea of the family homestead, to imagine a company owning so much land. There were many residents in the vicinity who could explain the Swan Company to them. Such people included William Booker, range foreman, cashier, and bookkeeper, who was fired along with John Clay in 1896 and who became manager of the Tolland Company. Duncan Grant, F. W. Lafrentz, Harry Haig—the brother of General Douglas Haig—and Fred Haight, who had managed the hotel for Swan but moved to Denver, where he managed the Cherry Hills Country Club until his death, could have told the story of the Swan Company.

According to a former Swan hand, it was a bunch of Two Bar cowhands who put on the impromptu rodeo in Cheyenne in 1896 that was the forerunner of the now famous Cheyenne Frontier Days celebration.[8] It was a Two Bar horse, named Muggins, who became so well known in rodeos and ranching that when he died he was buried in front of the administration building of the Los Angeles Stock Yards.[9]

There are other stories of the Two Bar, stories that become magnified with time but tend to enrich the heritage of the great company. Mrs. Virginia Wolff, wife of the present owner of the Two Bar at Wheatland, discovered a hanging tree on the ranch:

It seems that there was a **2** cowboy who was constantly late for meals at the cook house and then complained about the food when he did show up. The Chinese cook stood it

[8] Virginia Cole Trenholm, "Swan Song of the Two Bar," *Western Farm Life* (Denver), April 1, 1948, 5, 22.
[9] *Ibid.*

as long as he could and then hauled out his 6 shooter and shot the offending cowboy in the middle of his last complaint. The foreman told two of the men to hitch up the team and drive the cook to Cheyenne for trial. They had traveled only a few of the seventy-five miles when it began to snow. They reasoned that it was pretty silly to take him all that way just to be hung so they drove under the nearest cottonwood and hung him themselves, thus saving a lot of time and trouble.

The tree still stands on Sand Creek with a now unreadable legend carved on the main trunk and a hand with a finger pointing to the supporting limb.[10]

The bucking horse on the Wyoming license plate is believed to be a replica of old Steamboat, a famed bucking horse of the rodeos at the turn of the century. Steamboat was orginally a Two Bar horse, and the cowboys soon discovered that he could never be used as a cow horse, and so he became a rodeo horse. Steamboat was always wintered on the Two Bar. In 1914 he got blood poisoning from being torn up by a splintered corral post during an electrical storm. When it was learned that he would have to be shot, top cowboys from throughout the West gathered at Cheyenne to pay tribute to him.[11]

The famous cattle detective Tom Horn, according to his own story, came to Wyoming in 1894 and went to work for the Swan Company. There is no evidence that he was on the payroll, although John Clay, in his *My Life on the Range*, leaves little doubt that Horn was a frequent visitor to the Two Bar. Clay knew him well and described him vividly. Horn was later arrested and convicted of shooting

[10] Mrs. Virginia Wolff to author, July 31, 1970.
[11] *Ibid.*

a fourteen-year-old boy, Willie Nichol. Old-timers in Wheatland still argue the merits of the case.

Perhaps the best known of all Swan personalities was John Clay, shareholder, employee, manager, and director of the company. Clay and Murdo Mackenzie, of the Matador, are perhaps the two most-respected members of that fraternity of stockmen who managed the cattle empires of the American West. Clay's career can be best examined in *My Life on the Range*. Wherever Clay went, whether to Denver, Chicago, Kansas City, New York, Edinburgh, or London, so did the Swan Company.

One former employee has taken the time to put his remembrances of the Swan Company in print. A. S. ("Bud") Gillespie, a former cowhand for the Swan, thought that

> the Swan outfit was the best of all the cattle companies I have known. They furnished a variety of good food and plenty of it. They would butcher a beef about every third day, serve plenty of potatoes, beans, canned goods—about three kinds of canned goods—and three kinds of dried fruit, all washed down with plenty of good coffee. Suet pudding or rice and raisins were added for dessert.[12]

Not only was the food the best, so were the working conditions, wages, and opportunities: "When I was working for the Swan Land and Cattle Company they kept about 12 or 15 cowboys, including a foreman. . . . Also employed were a cook and a horse wrangler and a night wrangler."[13]

The company usually hired boys about nineteen years old at twenty dollars a month. If their work was satisfactory the cowboy could expect twenty-five dollars a month the

[12] A. S. ("Bud") Gillespie, "Reminiscences of a Swan Company Cowboy," *Annals of Wyoming* Vol. XXXVI (October, 1964), 220.
[13] *Ibid.*, 199.

second year, thirty dollars the third, and forty dollars the fourth. The two men with seniority in the company were paid forty-five dollars a month, and the foremen seventy-five dollars. Each rider was expected to furnish his own equipment, and the company provided him with a string of nine horses.

While a cowboy could feel secure and fortunate in his job with the Swan Company, he could also take pride in the brand he represented. Wrote Gillespie: "They never shipped a steer until he was fat and smoothed up if they had to keep him until he was seven or eight years old. They had to be beef."[14]

For over sixty years the Swan Company set the way of life and made several fortunes in Wyoming. The Two Bar was synonymous with good beef, a good life, and opportunity. Sheep seemed to dim the image somewhat, at least for a few years. Most people like to recall the days of the cattle, and especially of the open-range industry. Sheep were not anathema, but neither were they as romantic as cattle. The sheepherder with only his dogs and flocks for company just was not the romantic figure that the cowboy on horseback was.

Although the Swan Company no longer exists in reality, its image is still plain. The headquarters ranch with the old hotel—now a ranch house—the cashier and bookkeeper's house, the old store, and the barn are all intact just outside Chugwater, Wyoming. Down the road a short distance is Hi Kelly's old place, and so on across the range the landmarks appear. Russell Staats can still be found in the cashier's office handling the few affairs of the "Swan Company" of Wyoming, which is concerned with certain min-

[14] *Ibid.*, 199–201.

eral rights, and even it will cease to exist soon. Curtis Templin, the last manager and owner of the ranch, made his home at the Chugwater ranch until his death on December 28, 1968. In the evening one can stand outside the old ranch headquarters, and the sights and sounds of white-faced cattle and woolly sheep pass briefly across the mind. And one wishes the image would linger a little longer.

APPENDICES

Appendix A

OFFICERS OF SWAN LAND AND CATTLE COMPANY, LTD., 1883[1]

Directors:

Colin J. Mackenzie, Esq., of Portmore (Director of the British Linen Company Bank), Chairman.

Lord Douglas Gordon, M.P., London.

William Anderson, Esq., chartered accountant, Glasgow.

Hugh Beckett, Esq., Glasgow (Director of Nobel's Explosives Company, Limited).

James Shepherd, Esq., Manufacturer.

James Wilson, Esq., Edinburgh, formerly Merchant, China.

Alexander H. Swan, Esq., Cheyenne, Wyoming, U.S.A. (Will join the Board after the transfer of the Property.)

Bankers:

The British Linen Company Bank, Edinburgh, 41 Lombard Street, London, E.C. and Branches.

[1] "Report of the First General Meeting," July 30, 1883, Swan Collection, WRCIS.

Brokers:

Messrs. Bell, Begg, & Cowan, 8 North St. David Street, Edinburgh.

Messrs. Kerr, Andersons, Muir, & Main, 149 West George Street, Glasgow.

Solicitors:

Messrs. Fraser, Stodart, & Ballingall, W.S., 16 Castle Street, Edinburgh.

Auditors:

Messrs. Howden & Molleson, C.A., 5 North St. David Street, Edinburgh.

Manager in America:

Alexander H. Swan, Esq., Cheyenne.

Secretary:

Finlay Dun

Appendix B

Firm	Date of incorporation	Capitalization or estimated value
Cheyenne Driving Park Association	ca. 1880	None given
Swan Brothers	January 6, 1880	None given
Swan & Frank Live Stock Company	February 26, 1881	$ 648,000
National Cattle Company	July 16, 1881	550,000
Cheyenne Leader (Swan et al.)	October 1, 1881	6,000
Swan, Frank and Anthony Cattle Company	August 1, 1882	700,000

[1] Compiled from "Incorporation Records," WRCIS; Coutant Collection, Wyoming State Archives and Historical Department, Cheyenne; and Alexander Swan, 2d Collection, Western History Research Center, University of Wyoming, Laramie.

Ogallala Land and Cattle Company	December 20, 1882	5,000,000
Union Mercantile Company	May 16, 1883	120,000
Swan Land and Cattle Company, Ltd.	March 30, 1883	3,000,000
Wyoming Hereford Association	August 8, 1883	500,000
South Omaha Land Syndicate	August 20, 1883	1,000,000
	Estimated value, 1885	11,400,000
Cheyenne, Black Hills and Montana Railroad	November 10, 1883	10,000,000
Union Stock Yards Company of Omaha, Ltd.	December 1, 1883	1,000,000
Horse Creek Land and Cattle Company	December 4, 1883	200,000
Hillsdale Land and Cattle Company	November 6, 1884	500,000
Post Percheron Horse Association	August 6, 1885	1,000,000
Cheyenne Land and Live Stock Company	August 25, 1886	500,000
Ogden and Hot Springs Railway and Health Resort	ca. 1889	None given
White Swan Mining Company of Baker City, Utah	ca. 1889	None given
Iowa Stock Yards (Des Moines)	No date	350,000

Swan, Holmes and Company, Inc., Real Estate	No date	None given
Total Capital stock		$25,074,000

Appendix C

ABSTRACT OF LANDS OF SWAN LAND
AND CATTLE COMPANY, LTD., 1887[1]

Railway purchase (acres)			577,809
Other Lands			
I.	Titled		
	(a) Patent rights	6,303	
	(b) Final receipts	13,008	
			19,311
II.	Desert lands		
	(a) Acquired	17,418	
	(b) Relinquished	9,308	
			26,726
III.	Preemption lands		
	(a) Acquired	480	
	(b) Relinquished	600	
			1,080

[1] "Memorandum in Reference to Land Titles of the Swan Land and Cattle Company, Limited," July 11, 1887, Swan Files, WRCIS.

IV.	Homestead lands relinquished		160	
V.	Timber culture relinquished		961	
				48,238
				606,047

Total relinquished	11,029	
Total incomplete	17,898	
	28,927	28,927
Net total		577,120

Appendix D

DIVIDENDS PAID ON ORDINARY SHARES, 1883–1925,
SWAN LAND AND CATTLE COMPANY, LTD.[1]

Year	Amount of shares, pounds	Amount of dividend, per cent
1883	10	9
1884	10	10
1885	10	6
1886–96	10	None
1897[2]	2	5
1898	2	10
1899	2	12.5
1900	2	10
1901	2	7.5
1902	2	5
1903	2	None

[1] Annual reports and balance sheets, 1883–1925, Swan Collection, WRCIS.

[2] 1892 ordinary shares reduced from £10 to £2 by canceling £8 a share as not represented by available assets.

1904	2	2.5
1905	2	None
1906	2	2.5
1907	2	2.5
1908	2	None
1909	2	3.33
1910	2	5
1911–25	2	None

Appendix E

DIVIDENDS PAID ON STOCK, 1926–51.
SWAN COMPANY OF DELAWARE[1]

Year	Amount of shares dollars	Amount of dividend per cent	Bonds
1926–42	10.00[2]	None	Series A[3] Series B[4]
1943	10.00	None	Series A repaid
1944	10.00	None	Series B repaid 40%
1945	10.00	None	Series B repaid
1946	10.00	100 ($10.00 a share)	

[1] Annual reports and balance sheets, 1926–51, Swan Collection, WRCIS.

[2] 75,000 shares, $10 each ($75,000), not entitled to dividend until Series A repaid.

[3] Series A ($544,585) issued to 1924 debenture holders.

[4] Series B ($600,000) excess loan capital.

1947	10.00	20 ($2.00 a share)
1948	10.00	None
1949	10.00	None
1950	10.00	120[5]
1951	10.00	15.5[6]

[5] First distribution on liquidation.
[6] Final distribution on liquidation.

Appendix F

LIVESTOCK INVENTORY, 1883–1950, SWAN LAND AND
CATTLE COMPANY RECORDS, COURTESY CURTIS TEMPLIN
AND RUSSELL STAATS, NOVEMBER 3, 1955[1]

Year	Number of cattle	Number of horses	Number of sheep
1883	108,763	1,037	
1884	109,893	936	
1885	111,287	884	
1886	113,625	860	
1887	56,856	640	
1888	50,000	495	
1889	51,924	469	
1890	51,895	590	
1891	51,776	580	
1892	40,456	554	
1893	41,080	545	

[1] Burns, Gillespie, and Richardson, *Wyoming's Pioneer Ranches*,
508–10.

Year	Number of cattle	Number of horses	Number of sheep
1894	40,583	512	
1895	40,717	551	
1896	41,480	595	
1897	39,083	509	
1898	40,095	564	
1899	41,850	566	
1900	44,793	530	
1901	42,977	521	
1902	44,073	521	
1903	41,144	507	
1904	37,036	516	17,241
1905	32,571	482	42,106
1906	30,362	450	38,209
1907	29,073	453	60,870
1908	29,283	469	55,310
1909	27,879	453	62,298
1910	1,000	461	110,854
1911	542	360	112,365
1912	704	369	108,718
1913	1,442	312	101,898
1914	3,429	320	79,621
1915	3,472	387	64,787
1916	4,668	384	47,971
1917	1,155	356	52,633
1918	601	338	61,000
1919	275	295	48,454
1920	844	335	49,000
1921	201	327	58,500
1922	209	282	59,000
1923	190	261	54,500
1924	150	264	59,400

Year	Number of cattle	Number of horses	Number of sheep
1925	190	244	50,380
1926	227	243	55,400
1927	210	235	51,300
1928	218	231	56,800
1929	225	236	61,800
1930	236	236	73,800
1931	266	238	66,200
1932	189	225	61,900
1933	198	216	63,700
1934	116	214	71,900
1935	162	222	65,300
1936	106	212	67,700
1937	135	206	64,500
1938	159	210	66,100
1939	130	228	67,300
1940	145	230	60,800
1941	200	248	63,700
1942	233	263	58,100
1943	304	220	50,000
1944	310	173	40,000
1945	357	133	29,000
1946	365	65	13,600
1947	473	24	
1948	403	14	
1949	393	11	
1950			

Appendix G

RANCHES OWNED BY SWAN LAND AND CATTLE COMPANY, 1912[1]

A. L. Ranch
Bard Ranch
"Bates Hole"
Bear Creek Ranch
Beaver Dam Ranch
Bordeaux Ranch
Carlin Ranch
Chugwater Ranch
Chugwater Springs Ranch
C.M.D. Ranch
Diamond Ranch
Doty Ranch
49 Ranch
Greasewood Ranch
Harter Ranch
Jones Ranch

Kelly Ranch
Lone Tree Ranch
M Bar Ranch
Mule Shoe Ranch
Naffziger Ranch
Neilson Ranch
Peters Ranch (Nebraska)
Peters Ranch (Wyoming)
Seabourne Ranch
Shearing Pens Ranch
T. H. Ranch
Two Bar Ranch
T. Y. Ranch
Whitcomb Ranch
Y. B. O. Ranch
Yoder Ranch

[1] *Forman Report,* 1911–12. All the ranches listed above, evaluated as individual ranches, were in the possession of the Swan Company in 1912.

BIBLIOGRAPHY

The Swan Collection

The primary sources of this book are the papers of the Swan Land and Cattle Company, Ltd., in the Western Range Cattle Industry Study at the Colorado State Historical Society, Denver, Colorado.

Under a joint grant with the Library of Congress the State Historical Society of Colorado sent Herbert O. Brayer to the British Isles in the spring of 1947 to acquire all the available papers or copies of papers pertaining to British investment in the western cattle industry. The Swan Collection, which is the largest, was acquired through the services of Richard Gibson, of the law firm of Clay and Pringle, in Edinburgh. Gibson was the last secretary of the company and represented the Scottish investors after the company became an American corporation in 1927.

The collection consists primarily of the papers of William Fraser—the company's attorney, a member of the law firm of Fraser, Stodart, and Ballingall, of Edinburgh. It contains many of Fraser's drafts, memoranda, marginal comments, and recommendations. The remainder of the collection contains the Articles of Association, the bylaws, details of the corporate and financial structure from 1883 to 1927, annual financial reports, lists of stockholders, all court orders, the correspondence of the secretary, newspapers and journal clippings, legal decisions, and miscellaneous information, totaling about twelve thousand items.

The collection, with some unexplained exceptions, is arranged in chronological order, and any item cited can be found by examining the proper folder in the collection. The contents of this collection are also available on microfilm (fifteen reels). The collection was microfilmed when it was first acquired. At present, because of use and rearrangement, some items do not appear in the same order on the microfilm as they do in the files. Some microfilmed items are no longer in the collection (notably reel thirteen, which contains the printed annual reports and profit-and-loss statements for the years 1883–1944). Some materials which Brayer catalogued under the terms of the grant are neither in the collection nor on the microfilm.

All reference to Scottish newspapers and journals, British documents, and several legal papers are a part of the collection and are cited as such in the footnotes.

OTHER UNPUBLISHED MATERIAL

Cheyenne, Wyoming. Wyoming State Archives and Historical Department. C. G. Coutant Collection; Wilkerson Collection.

Laramie, Wyoming. Western History Research Center, University of Wyoming. James T. Craig Collection; F. W. Lafrentz Collection; Alexander Swan, 2d Collection; Wyoming Stock Growers' Association Collection.

PUBLIC DOCUMENTS

Richardson, J. D., ed. *Compilation of the Messages and Papers of the Presidents, 1789–1897.* 20 vols. 53d Cong., 2d sess.,

House Misc. Doc. No. 210, Parts 1–10. New York, Bureau of National Literature, Inc., 1897.

U.S. Congress. *Report of the Governor of Wyoming to the Secretary of Interior, November 23, 1885*, 49th Cong., 1st sess. (1885). Washington, Government Printing Office, 1886.

——. *Report of the Governor of Wyoming to the Secretary of Interior, 1887.* 50th Cong., 1st sess. (1888). Washington, Government Printing Office, 1888.

——. *Statutes of the United States of America*, 49th Cong., 2d sess., 1886–87, Chap. 340, pp. 476–77. "An Act to Restrict the Ownership of Real Estate in the Territories to American Citizens and So Forth." March 3, 1887.

——, House. *Fifteenth Annual Report of the Bureau of Animal Industry for the Year 1898.* "The Cattle Industry of Colorado, Wyoming, and Nevada and the Sheep Industry of Colorado in 1897," by John T. McNelly, 55th Cong., 3d sess. (1899), *House Doc. No. 307.*

——. *The Range and Ranch Cattle Business*, by Joseph Nimmo, Jr., 48th Cong., 2d sess. (1888), *House Doc. No. 267.*

——. *Report of the Acting Commissioner of the General Land Office on the Use of the Public Lands by Cattle Grazers*, 50th Cong., 1st sess. (1888), *House Ex. Doc. No. 232.*

——. *Report of the House Committee on Public Lands on the Ownership of Real Estate in Territories by Foreigners*, 49th Cong., 1st sess. (1886), *House Report No. 3445.*

——, Senate. *Communication of the Secretary of Interior to Congress with Accompanying Papers Urging the Necessity of Stringent Measures for the Repression of the Evasions and Violations of Laws Relating to the Public Lands*, 47th Cong., 2d sess. (1883), *Sen. Ex. Doc. No. 61.*

——. *Report of the Commissioner of the General Land Office on the Unauthorized Fencing of Public Lands*, 48th Cong., 1st sess. (1884), *Sen. Ex. Doc. No. 127.*

———. Report of the Treasury Cattle Commission on Lung Plague of Cattle or Contagious Pleuro-Pneumonia, 47th Cong., 1st sess. (1882), Sen. Ex. Doc. 106.

———. Testimony Taken by the Select Committee of the U.S. Senate on the Transportation and Sale of Meat Products, 51st Cong., 1st sess. (1890), Sen. Rept. 829.

U.S. Statutes at Large, Vol. XXXIX, Part 1 (December, 1915–March, 1917). Public Law No. 290. "An Act to Provide for Stock-raising Homesteads and for Other Purposes."

COURT CASES

Swan Land and Cattle Company vs. Joseph Frank et al. 148 U.S. 603.

Swan Land and Cattle Company vs. Peter Pompel. District Court. Carbon County, Rawlins, Wyoming. (Eight cases filed between September 5, 1885, and August 17, 1891, Doc. Nos. 401, 453, 483, 558, 559, 560, 563, 568.)

Swan Land and Cattle Co., Limited vs. Frank et al. 39 Fed. Rept. 461.

United States of America vs. Alexander Swan. November, 1884, Laramie County, Wyoming, Chancery Docket, No. 45.

United States of America vs. Alexander Swan, Thomas Swan, Zachariah Thomason and Charles S. Anthony. November, 1885, Laramie County, Wyoming Territory, Chancery Docket No. 1-45.

United States of America vs. Hiram B. Kelly. November, 1885. Laramie County, Wyoming Territory, Chancery Docket No. 1-70.

United States of America vs. John Hunton. November, 1885, Laramie County, Wyoming Territory, Chancery Docket No. 1-69.

INTERVIEWS

Staats, Russell. Cashier of the Swan Land and Cattle Company,

Ltd., since 1924. Chugwater, Wyoming. July 18, 1968.

Swan, Henry. Nephew of Alexander Swan, former director and treasurer of State Historical Society of Colorado, director and vice-president of United States National Bank of Denver, and trustee of the University of Denver. Denver, Colorado, August 13, 1967.

Templin, Curtis. Manager of the Swan Land and Cattle Company, Ltd., since 1915. Cheyenne, Wyoming, August 21, 1968.

NEWSPAPERS

Carbon County Journal (Rawlins, Wyoming), October, 1880–January, 1886.

Cheyenne (Wyoming) *Daily Leader*, November, 1887.

Cheyenne (Wyoming) *Sun*, August–November, 1883.

Daily Boomerang (Laramie, Wyoming), July–December, 1886.

Kansas City (Missouri) *Livestock Indicator*, April–November, 1887.

Omaha Daily Journal Stockman, January, 1931.

Wheatland (Wyoming) *Times*, August, 1933.

Wyoming State Tribune (Cheyenne), March, 1960.

ARTICLES

Brayer, Herbert O. "The Influence of British Capital on the Western Range Cattle Industry," *Westerners' Brand Book* (Denver), Vol. IV (May, 1948), 1–19.

Brayer, Herbert O. "The L7 Ranches: An Incident in the Economic Development of the Western Cattle Industry," *Annals of Wyoming*, Vol. XV (January, 1943), 5–37.

Brayer, Herbert O. "Moreton Frewen, Cattleman," *Westerners' Brand Book* (Denver), Vol. V (July, 1949).

Brayer, Herbert O. "The 76 Ranch on the Powder River," *West-*

erners' Brand Book (Chicago), Vol. VII (December, 1950), 1ff.

Clements, Roger V. "British-controlled Enterprise in the West Between 1870 and 1900, and Some Agrarian Reactions," *Agricultural History*, Vol. XXVII (October, 1953), 132–41.

Clements, Roger V. "British Investment and American Legislative Restrictions in the Trans-Mississippi West, 1880–1900," *Mississippi Valley Historical Review*, Vol. XLII (September, 1955), 207-28.

Collins, Dabney Otis. "In the Tracks of the Two Bar Wagon," *Record Stockman*, Annual Edition, 1954, 55ff.

Gillespie, A. S. "Reminiscences of a Swan Company Cowboy," *Annals of Wyoming*, Vol. XXXVI, No. 2 (October, 1964), 198–221.

Grohman, W. Baillie. "Cattle Ranches in the Far West," *The Fortnightly Review*, Vol. XXVIII (N.S., July–December, 1880), 438–57.

Jackson, W. Turrentine. "The Wyoming Stock Growers' Association: Political Power in Wyoming Territory, 1873–1890," *Mississippi Valley Historical Review*, Vol. XXXIII (March, 1947), 571–94.

Jackson, W. Turrentine. "Railroad Relations of the Wyoming Stock Growers' Association, 1873–1890," *Annals of Wyoming*, Vol. XIV (January, 1942), 3–23.

Larson, T. A. "The Winter of 1886–87 in Wyoming," *Annals of Wyoming*, Vol. XIV (January, 1942), 5–17.

Mattison, Ray H. "The Hard Winter and the Range Cattle Business," *The Montana Magazine of History*, Vol. I (October, 1951), 14–26.

Scottish Banking and Insurance Magazine, Financial Record, Economic and Railway Review, April 7, 1883, 80.

Smith, Helena Huntington. "The Rise and Fall of Alec Swan," *The American West*, Vol. IV (August, 1967), 21ff.

Thompson, Albert W. "The Great Prairie Cattle Company, Ltd.,"
    The Colorado Magazine, Vol. II (March, 1945), 76–83.
Trenholm, Virginia Cole. "Swan Song of the Two Bar," *Western
    Farm Life*, April 1, 1948, 5ff.

BOOKS

Athearn, Robert G. *High Country Empire*. New York, McGraw-
    Hill Book Company, Inc., 1960.
Athearn, Robert G. *Westward the Briton*. New York, Charles
    Scribner's Sons, 1953.
Atherton, Louis. *The Cattle Kings*. Bloomington, Indiana Uni-
    versity Press, 1961.
Bancroft, Hubert Howe. *History of Nevada, Colorado and Wyo-
    ming*. San Francisco, The History Company Publishers,
    1890.
Bray, Charles. *Financing the Western Cattle Industry*, Colorado
    Agricultural College *Bulletin* 338. Fort Collins, 1928.
Burns, Robert H., Andrew S. Gillespie, and William C. Richard-
    son. *Wyoming's Pioneer Ranches*. Laramie, Top-of-the-
    World Press, 1932.
Clapham, J. H. *An Economic History of Modern Britain: Free
    Trade and Steel, 1850–1886*. 2 vols. Cambridge, Cambridge
    University Press, 1932.
Clay, John. *My Life on the Range*. Norman, University of Okla-
    homa Press, 1962.
Dale, Edward Everett. *Cow Country*. Norman, University of
    Oklahoma Press, 1965.
Dale, Edward Everett. *The Range Cattle Industry, 1865–1925*.
    Norman, University of Oklahoma Press, 1960.
Fletcher, Robert H. *Free Grass to Fences, the Montana Cattle
    Range Story*. New York, University Publishers, 1960.
Frink, Maurice, W. Turrentine Jackson, and Agnes Wright
    Spring. *When Grass Was King*. Boulder, University of Colo-
    rado Press, 1956.

Gressley, Gene M. *Bankers and Cattlemen.* New York, Alfred A. Knopf, 1966.

Jackson, W. Turrentine. *The Enterprising Scot.* Edinburgh, Edinburgh University Press, 1968.

Jenks, Leland H. *The Migration of British Capital to 1875.* London, Jonathan Cape, 1938.

Larmer, Forrest M. *Financing the Livestock Industry.* New York, The Macmillan Company, 1926.

Latham, Hirm. *Trans-Missouri Stock Raising: The Pasture Lands of North America: Winter Grazing.* Denver, Old West Publishing Company, 1962.

McCoy, Joseph G. *Historic Sketches of the Cattle Trade of the West and Southwest.* Ed. by Ralph B. Bieber. Glendale, Arthur H. Clark Company, 1940.

MacDonald, James. *Food from the Far West.* Edinburgh, W. P. Nimmo, 1878.

Nordyke, Lewis. *Great Roundup: The Story of Texas and Southwestern Cowmen.* New York, William Morrow, 1949.

Oliphant, J. Orin. *On The Cattle Ranges of the Oregon Country.* Seattle, University of Washington Press, 1968.

Osgood, Ernest Staples. *The Day of the Cattlemen.* Minneapolis, University of Minnesota Press. 1929.

Peake, Ora B. *The Colorado Range Cattle Industry.* Glendale, Arthur H. Clark Company, 1937.

Pearce, W. M. *The Matador Land and Cattle Company.* Norman, University of Oklahoma Press, 1964.

Pelzer, Louis. *The Cattlemen's Frontier.* Glendale, Arthur H. Clark Company, 1936.

Savage, James W., and John T. Bell. *City of Omaha Nebraska and South Omaha.* New York, Munsell & Company, 1894.

Schlebecker, John T. *Cattle Raising on the Plains 1900–1961.* Lincoln, University of Nebraska Press, 1963.

Spence, Clark C. *British Investment and the American Mining Frontier.* Ithaca, Cornell University Press, 1958.

Webb, Walter Prescott. *The Great Plains.* New York, Grossett & Dunlap, 1931.

Wentworth, Edward Norris. *America's Sheep Trails.* Ames, University of Iowa Press, 1948.

Wyoming: The 75th Year. Douglas, June, 1965.

INDEX

Abilene, Kans.: 6
Adams, John: 73
Agassiz, Louis: 10
Alien Land Act: 73, 93; of 1886–87, 113–14
A. L. Ranch, reservoir on: 127
American Beef Trust: 16
Ames, Frederick L.: 120
Anderson, L. M.: 56, 57
Anthony, Charles E.: 37, 38, 55
Apperson, John A.: 81
Armour, Philip: 88

Badger Lake, irrigation near: 128
Bard Ranch, sale of: 157
Book count (cattle): 30
Booker, William: 167
Bosler, Joseph: 57
Boulter, C.: 55
Bowie, Al: 41, 81, 103, 104, 135
British investment: 7, 13, 15; in 1882, 16–17; in 1886, 89
British press: 14–15; warns against speculation, 28–29

California gold rush (1849): 13
Carey, Joseph M.: 49, 166

Carlson Ranch: 157
Cattle: types of, 24; losses of, 1886–87, 75–76; overstocking of, 88; government report on, 1893, 91–92; prices of, 1884–88, 100; quality of, 165; see also cattle trade, herd losses
Cattle trade: on High Plains, 4, 5; in the 1870's, 8; problems in, during 1880's, 16
Cherokee Strip Livestock Association: 112
Cheyenne, Black Hills, Montana Railroad: 58
Cheyenne, Wyo., trade, in 1875: 7
Chugwater Creek: 40
Chugwater, Wyo.: 135–36
Clay, A. Thomson: 135
Clay, John: 50–51, 151, 161; selected as manager, 103; range policy of, 104; dismissal of, 105; on financial changes, 109; as member of board, 135; as member of American executive committee, 135–36; proposes transfer of company to United States, 149
Cleveland, President Grover: 112

Colorado and Southern Railway: 136
CMD Ranch: 157
Converse, James: 17, 37
Corlett, William, report of, on land titles: 27, 73
Craig, James T.: 133, 136, 151; as range manager, 135; as member of American executive committee, 135
Creighton, John A.: 57

Dawson, William: 135
Day, Mabel: 10
Diseases, cattle: Texas fever, 6; anthrax, 14; pleuropneumonia, 16
Drimmie, Thomas: as cause of Swan Brothers' failure, 67; as shareholder, 68
Dry farmers: 117, 123, 130
Dun, Finlay: 37; on investments in America, 30; on Wyoming Stock Growers' Association, 52; as interim manager, 65–66; as candidate for manager, 101; see also Dun Report
Dun Report (Finlay): on failure of Swan Brothers, 71; and notes by A. H. Swan on company, 71; on debts owed to company, 72; recommends embezzlement charges, 72; on land titles, 72–73; on Union Pacific lands, 74; on trespasses, 75; on cattle count of 1887, 75; on herd losses of 1886–87, 76; on changes in ranch management, 81; on suggested changes in company management, 82

Eastern investment: 9, 10
Ellwood, Isaac: 12

Fairfield, George W.: 114
Foreign investment: 11
Forman, George, report on lands:

on plains section, 124–25; on land evaluation, 125; on Elk Mountain, 126; on land use, 126; on irrigation, 127–29; on Goshen Hole, 129; summary of, 129–30
Frank, Joseph: 17, 37, 38, 71, 73, 79
Fraser, William: 33, 64, 108
Frewen, Moreton: 51–52

Gillespie, A. S.: 169
Goshen Hole, Wyo.: 127, 128, 130
Grant, Duncan: 167
Grohman, W. Baillie: 15
Guthrie, W. E.: 165

Haggard, Avery: 154
Haig, Harry: 167
Herd books: 25
Herd growth: in original herds, 24–25; estimates of, 1882–90, 42; distribution of, 1888, 86; estimates of, 1887, 94
Herd losses: 61; and cattle count of, 1887, 75; in 1886–87, 75–76, 163; see also Dun Report
Herefords: 24, 54; importation of, 55
Horn, Tom: 168–69
Hoyt, Gov. John W.: 23

Iler, Peter E.: 57
Iowa Land and Thoroughbred Livestock Association: 65

John Clay and Company: 131
Johnson, Frank M.: 127
Johnson, M. R.: 135, 136
Johnson County War: 53
Johnston, James C.: report of, on cattle, 1887, 78; recommendations of, on range management, 87; as candidate for manager, 101; as chairman of board, 131, 136; on retaining of livestock,

134; on reorganization in 1923–24, 146

Kelly, Hiran B. ("Hi"): 39, 115
Kendrick, John B.: 166
Kingman Ranch: 55

Lafrentz, Frederick W.: 56, 68, 167
Lake Ione, irrigation near: 129
Land: original holdings of, 22–23; disputed titles to, 73–74; value of, in 1887, 94; disposal of, 131; accounting of, 1917, 134; Wyoming state, 147; efforts to dispose of, 152; sales of, 1943–50, 157–58; *see also* Union Pacific; Forman, George, report on lands; Lawson, Thomas
Landale, Thomas: attack of, on directors, 93; and shareholder's committee report, 94–95; elected to board, 100
Lawson, Thomas: 67; report of, on lands and ranches, 19–22, 26; letter from, in regard to A. H. Swan, 70; letter from, to shareholders, 96–97; on herd losses, 1886–87, 97; on company management, 97; on Finlay Dun, 98; on use of calf brands, 1883–87, 99
LD Ranch: 158

McCoy, Joseph G.: 6
MacDonald, James: 15
Mackenzie, Colin: 37, 57, 97, 137; report of, on ranches, 39–40; on ranch communications, 40–41
Mackenzie, Murdo: 169
McNab, Alexander, Jr.: 33; as member of board, 100; opposition of, to sale of land, 133; as chairman, 135
McShane, John A.: 57
Matador Land and Cattle Company: 160, 162

Mavericks, and Wyoming Stock Growers' Association bill: 51–52
M Bar Ranch: irrigation of, 128, 130; sale of, 158
Menzies, William John: 108
Missouri Land and Live Stock Company: 67
Moonlight, Gov. Thomas: 88
Morgan, George F.: 55
Mormons: 5
Morris, Nelson: 10
Muleshoe Ranch: 40, 157
Murphy, Frank: 57
Murray, Thomas: 135
Myers, John W.: 166

Nagle, Erasmus: 71
Naffziger Ranch: 158
National Cattle Company: 19, 25, 34
Neilson Ranch: 139, 157

Open range: problems of, 114; fencing of, 115–16; and dry farmers, 130; closing of, 130
Oregon Trail: 3
Overstocking: *see* herd losses

Paxton, W. A.: 56, 57
Payson, Rep. Lewis E.: 113
Peters Ranch: 128
Pompell, Peter: 74
Post, M. E.: 49
Prairie Cattle Company: 17, 160, 162
Prentice, George, Jr.: 82, 97; report of, on properties, 1883, 37–38; as chairman of board, 135

Railroads: 6, 7; significance of, 7; *see also* Union Pacific Railroad
Ranches: improvement of, 139; cost of operations of, 140; *see also* under individual ranches; *Forman Report*
Reel Herd: 93

Rehmeyer Ranch: 39
Rhodes, Rufus: as ranch foreman, 41; buys "07" Ranch, 72; on wintering herds, 85
Richard Creek: 40

Scottish American Mortgage Company: 17, 107
Searight Brothers: 24
Shearing Pens Ranch: 129, 158
Sheep: trespasses by, 74; introduction of, 123; prices for, 1911–12, 124; wool of, 1911–12, 124; war prices for, 132–33; prices for, 1919–20, 148
Shephard Reservoir: 127
Shepherd, James: 135
Smith, J. Duncan: 17
Snydacker, Godfrey: 9, 17, 37
South Omaha Land Syndicate (Nebraska): 56
Staats, Russell: 170
Standard Cattle Company: 40
Sturgis, Thomas: 45, 50–51; views of, on British investors, 90–91
Swan, Alexander: 55, 71; in Wyoming Territory, 17; and organization of original companies, 19–22, 32; introduction of Herefords by, 24; on origin of herds, 24; on calf brands, 33; as manager, 37; on original shares, 37; negotiations of, for Union Pacific lands, 41; estimate of, on herd growth, 1883–90, 42; arrival of, in Wyoming, 45–46; early background of, 46; and formation of Swan Brothers, 46; joins Wyoming Stock Growers' Association, 48; political offices of, 48–49; conflict of, with Wyoming Stock Growers' Association, 50–52; on maverick bill, 51–52; founds South Omaha (Nebr.) and Union Stock Yards, 56–57; other business enterprises of, 58;

embezzlement charges against, 72; as party in case against vendors, 79–80; and purchase of Union Pacific lands, 117–18; election of, to Cowboy Hall of Fame, 165–66
Swan, Frank and Anthony Cattle Company: 19, 25, 35
Swan, Henry (father): 47, 48
Swan, Thomas (brother): 17, 47, 55
Swan, Thomas (Scots shareholder): 100
Swan, Will F. (brother): 47, 48
Swan and Frank Live Stock Company: 19, 25, 32, 35
Swan Brothers: 25, 60; founded, 46; purchase by, of Herefords, 54–55; failure of, 64–67
Swan Company of Delaware: transfer of assets of, 153; capital structure of, 153; change of name of, 154; foreign-company status of, 154; organization of, 155; first annual report of, 156; land sales of, 1943–50, 157–58; liquidation of, 158–59
Swan Company of Wyoming: 170
Swan Land and Cattle Company: 72; original companies of, 19–22; initial agreements of, 34; original capitalization of, 35–36; board of directors of, 36–37; share distribution of, 37; capital increase of, 1886, 92; reorganization scheme of, 1891–92, 106; capital reduction of, 1898, 110; eastern division lands of, 117; land titles of, 120–21; board reorganization of, 135; financial status of, 1917, 142–43; reorganization scheme of, 1917, 144–45; reorganization scheme of, 1923–24, 146–47; income taxes of, 149; transfer of, to United States, 151; final report of, 156; financial returns

of, 162; and ranch life, 166, 169; personnel of, 167, 169–70

Swan Land and Cattle Company Limited vs. *Joseph Frank, et al.*: 79

Swift, William: employed for vendor's suit, 64; case of, against vendors, 79–80; on future of cattle business, 101–102; recommends John Clay as manager, 102; and proposed land case, 121

Swobe, Thomas: 57

Sybille Creek: 40

Tait, James: report and recommendations of, 1884, 62; recommends suit against vendors, 63; as member of Missouri Land and Live Stock Company, 67; recommendations of, on range management, 86

Templin, Curtis: 151; joins company, 136–37; as manager, 137; reports of, 137–40; efforts of, to change name and residence of company, 154–55; gift of ranch to, 158

Texas cattle: losses of, in 1884–86, 61; losses of, in 1887, 77, 164

Texas longhorns: 6

Thomason, Zack: 69

Thorp, Russell: 56

T. H. Ranch: 157

Two Bar Ranch: 138, 139; sale of,

157; and Frontier Days Celebration, 167

Underwood, Clark and Company: 17

Union Mercantile Company: 58

Union Pacific Railroad, lands of: 41, 74, 92, 108, 117–18, 122–23

Union Stock Yards (Omaha): 54–57

United States Bureau of Animal Husbandry: 91

Urquhart, Robert: applies for company positions, 68, 101; as critic of Swan, 69; and letter from Lawson about A. H. Swan, 69–70

Vendor's suit: 79–80

Warren, Francis E.: 45, 166

Watson, John Guthrie, report of, on company: 107–108

Weather: 16, 30, 76, 138

Whitcomb Ranch: 39, 157

Wilson, James: 29, 32

Woolworth, J. W.: 80, 116

Wyoming Hereford Association: 54, 55, 71

Wyoming Stock Growers' Association: A. H. Swan as president of, 48–49; political power of, 50; and maverick bill, 51–52